EAT YOUR FEELINGS

EAT YOUR FEELINGS

How to Devour, Digest, and Detox Pain From Your Life

Cristina P Simmons

©2025 All Rights Reserved. No portion of this book may be reproduced, stored in a retrieval system, or transmitted in any form or by any means—electronic, mechanical, photocopy, recording, scanning, or other—except for brief quotations in critical reviews or articles without the prior permission of the author.

Published by Game Changer Publishing

Paperback ISBN: 978-1-967424-88-7

Hardcover ISBN: 978-1-967424-91-7

Digital ISBN: 978-1-967424-92-4

www.GameChangerPublishing.com

*I dedicate this book to Dani, Dori, and Juddsen—
my angels here on earth.*

*Also to my guardian angels in Heaven: Kaelynn, Kadyn, and DJ.
You all gave me the most cherished opportunity I could
have ever asked for—being your mother.*

READ THIS FIRST

Just to say thanks for buying and reading my book,
I would love to connect with you!

Scan the QR Code Here:

EAT YOUR FEELINGS

HOW TO DEVOUR, DIGEST, AND DETOX PAIN FROM YOUR LIFE

CRISTINA P SIMMONS

FOREWORD

It's one thing to live through trauma.

It's another thing entirely to write about it.

To revisit every wound.

To unwrap every scar.

To face the parts of your story that once left you breathless, broken, and buried under shame—and still choose to say: *This might help someone else heal.*

That's the kind of courage you'll find in these pages.

Eat Your Feelings is not just a book—it's a lifeline. It's a brave, beautifully written, unfiltered invitation into the raw and real places most people spend their whole lives trying to hide. With each chapter, the author doesn't just tell her truth—she *owns* it, and in doing so, she gives others permission to own theirs too.

As I read her words, I found myself stunned—not just by what she survived, but by how fiercely she chose to *rise*. Her voice is one of resilience, yes—but also of relentless love. A love that fought for her children, for her marriage, for her health, for her wholeness, and eventually, for herself. A love that shows up in these stories—not wrapped in a bow, but poured out in real, messy, honest humanity.

FOREWORD

What moved me most is that she didn't write this from a mountaintop of "having arrived." She wrote it from the trenches. From the place where healing is still happening. From the sacred space of "me too," where empathy lives and hope takes root.

She shows us that trauma doesn't have to have the final say. That grief doesn't get to write the whole story. That we are not defined by what happened to us, but by how we rise from it, grow through it, and use it to serve others.

There is a wisdom in this book that only comes from lived experience. From sitting in the pain and doing the hard work of digesting —not avoiding—life's most difficult truths. The frameworks she shares aren't theories. They're battle-tested. They were built in hospital rooms, in tear-soaked prayers, in therapy sessions, in sleepless nights, in conversations with God, and in the quiet moments when she chose *not* to give up.

This book will meet you where you are—and gently lead you somewhere better. Not with judgment, but with grace. Not with a blueprint, but with an open hand. You'll laugh in parts. You'll cry in others. But more than anything, you'll finish it knowing that healing is possible, and that you don't have to walk through it alone.

Your words will set people free.

And to the reader: Get ready.

This is not just a book you read—it's one you *experience*.

Let it reach the parts of you that you've buried. Let it open doors you didn't realize were still locked. Let it show you that the very feelings you've been avoiding might just be the key to your greatest transformation.

With deep admiration,
– Amberly Lago
Speaker | Author of *True Grit and Grace*
and *Joy Through the Journey*

CONTENTS

INTRODUCTION	xiii
1. PRIDE PIE *(Bittersweet Dark Chocolate)*	1
2. MARRIAGE *(Hot Honey Barbecue Wings)*	13
3. KAELYNN ALECIA, MARCH 26–29, 2002 *(Strawberry Shortcake)*	25
4. MISCARRIAGE *(Sour Grapes)*	37
5. KADYN, THE TASTE OF HOPE *(Warm Vanilla Custard)*	45
6. GRIEF, ANXIETY, AND DEPRESSION *(Salt and Vinegar Chips—The Whole Bag)*	55
7. DANI AND DORI *(Christmas Cookies)*	65
8. DJ: DONNIE JR. *(Salted Caramel Cheesecake)*	75
9. JUDDSEN *(Gluten-Free Pizza)*	81
10. AUTISM *(Gummy Worms, No Artificial Flavors)*	85
11. CANCER *(Stale Saltine Crackers)*	99
12. E.A.T. (EDUCATE-ACCEPT-TRANSFORM) *(Chicken Vegetable Soup)*	109
13. THE F.O.O.D. FRAMEWORK *(Stuffed Bell Peppers)*	119
14. THIS IS NOT THE LAST CHAPTER *(Pineapple Upside Down Cake)*	127
ACKNOWLEDGMENTS	129
THANK YOU FOR READING MY BOOK!	131

INTRODUCTION

Have you ever heard one of those stories that you couldn't believe? A story that seemed too incredible to be true or too awful to fathom? A story of a family that had endured heartbreak after heartbreak—but also miracle after miracle?

These are the kinds of stories that happen to other people, not you. These are the kinds of stories that prayer chains are made of.

Sometimes, when I tell our story, it feels like I'm talking about someone else, like I watched it from afar, because I was dissociated. The Mayo Clinic defines dissociation as a "disconnection and lack of continuity between thoughts, memories, surroundings, actions, and identity." If I disconnected from my thoughts, I wouldn't have to remember. My surroundings didn't have to dictate the actions or lack of action that I took, and I didn't have an identity, because I couldn't figure out who I really was or even who I longed to be.

Have you been faced with grief, broken dreams, lost relationships, heartache that you aren't sure you can recover from, or debilitating anxiety, overwhelm, or depression? These have been some of my struggles, and I realize now that I am not alone. So, I wrote this

INTRODUCTION

book for you—to help you heal, to help you deal, to help you feel again.

But most of all, I wrote it for myself. To help me finally close the once gaping hole deep inside my spirit. I used to try to fill it with food, but it never completely satisfied me; I always felt empty, no matter how much I ate.

Eating was also so much easier than processing. Eating provides instant gratification and input to the senses. I used to joke that my nerves were shot. The nervous system instinctively tries to reroute pain and discomfort as a protective mechanism. Whenever I'm anxious, I want something crunchy or salty or crunchy and salty. Crunching provides sensory feedback in your mouth, which takes the mind off of whatever it is I am trying to avoid. I also crave working out. I need to move my body. I need to pick up heavy weights and put them down repeatedly. I share more about this in Chapter 10: My son with autism likes weighted items and loves roller coasters. It sounds crazy, but G-force calms him.

When I'm sad, I want something sweet, or something with a pudding consistency, or cake, dare I say *moist*? But if I'm angry, I want comfort food—something hot, something warm and hearty, like chili or a thick soup.

I've been on quite a journey, and I have developed many coping mechanisms along the way. Walk along with me on the path to healing because I need to get this out. I need to feel all the emotions, digest how my circumstances have changed my life (both good and bad), and then purge what no longer serves me.

By the end of this book, you will be equipped with strategies, new frameworks, and tools that you can return to again and again and implement when faced with your own obstacles. I have been stuffing my soul for decades, keeping all of the things I thought were shameful, guiltful, hurtful, and hateful all down in my gut, where they are now seeping out into my system. I can't keep them there

INTRODUCTION

anymore, festering away and slowly killing me, both mentally and physically.

I recently found out that I have symptoms and markers for SIBO, IBS, IBD, malabsorption, liver imbalance, an overall inflammatory bowel, leaky gut, high cholesterol, low immunity, and pre-diabetes. These all put me at risk for a cardiac event (attack or stroke), Alzheimer's, Diabetes, and a host of other illnesses. I have been on the path to wellness for a good part of fifteen years now: eating clean whenever possible, drinking lots of water, taking all the supplements, reading all the books, listening to all the podcasts. These are all outside sources, but are not the root of the problem.

While I have been feeding my body nutritious meals and praying all the while, my soul never wholeheartedly believed that I could feel good and live pain free. I have been conditioned to self-sabotage and run from my responsibilities, all the while ensuring everyone else was happy and striving to be an overachiever to prove my worth. At the age of 48, I still feel like a child who needs someone to tell her what to do, how to think, and when she can speak. I am tired of living like that; I am tired of not feeling well; I am tired of not having the freedom to live this life the way I truly want to. I am still not sure where to start my story, but as the saying goes, we all have to start somewhere.

Some of my memories seem like they belong to other people. Like my mom or dad told me, "about a time when," so I took it as a memory of my own. I have a few memories from around the age of five, or possibly even younger. My family has always had an inside joke about my dad not being very handy around the house. He would also sweat profusely with any sort of physical exertion. So the inside joke was that whenever he was sweating, we would ask, "Did Dad just pick up a hammer?" Because no matter what he was doing, he was sweating. Kind of like Forrest Gump, whenever he was going somewhere, he "was running."

So, when I was about three or four years old, Dad was trying to

INTRODUCTION

fix something in the basement. This was when we lived in Michigan for a while. I was helping, and whenever Dad would ask for a tool, I would run and get it.

Dad would say, "I need a hammer."

I would reply, "Hammer! Coming right up!"

Cute, right? One of those endearing moments between father and daughter, where you might guess that they were lifelong pals and ended up going into business together and living happily ever after. Well, this is not that story.

I am fairly certain that this encounter marked the moment when we both unconsciously entered into an agreement: He told me what to do, and I either followed through with a "coming right up!" or I failed to live up to his standards, which resulted in verbal and occasional physical abuse.

His standards were pretty high. My ability to live up to them was pretty low, at least according to how often he screamed at me, made sure I knew that any idea I had was stupid, and asserted that only he knew anything about everything, while everyone else was extremely uneducated. My capacity to endure mental abuse expanded. My confidence in myself waned. We didn't get a happy ever after.

I am going to share more of the stories that have shaped who I am today. The ones I told myself were true and the ones that proved to be false.

I also want to share my frameworks for overcoming those stories. Each of these was born through prayer and inner work. I developed the acronyms in 2024, but I had been using the principles for years without even knowing it. We will work through the following methods:

- **S.A.F.E.** This will shift your perspective.
- **C.A.L.M.** We have used to navigate Autism and sensory processing with my son, as well as other families I have worked with in the past and present.

INTRODUCTION

- **E.A.T**. The primary tool I used to persevere through traumatic events and situations.
- **F.O.O.D. Framework.** This has enabled me to cultivate a healthier relationship with food, both mentally and physically

My hope and prayer is that my personal stories of perseverance and the tools that my family has used to navigate life's darkest times can give you comfort and the knowledge to gain the courage to take back your power.

CHAPTER 1
PRIDE PIE
(BITTERSWEET DARK CHOCOLATE)

I avoided looking myself in the eye for the last twenty years, living on autopilot for over two decades. It's quite impressive the amount I've accomplished in survival mode. Just imagine what I can do fully present, feeling worthy, and finally free of trauma symptoms that kept me in a fog for so long. I check out of certain situations, make a U-turn when conflict arises, clam up when I should be verbally vomiting my feelings, and love to tell or hear anyone else's story rather than my own.

I was the girl who never felt like she fit in, and the woman who still feels left out. I was the girl who only talked to God about her feelings and the woman who still feels alone in a crowded room. I was the girl who always felt less than, and the woman who now overachieves to feel like she's enough. I was the girl who had to grow up fast and the woman who thinks she needs to fix everyone else's problems. If you focus on everyone else, your problems will just go away, right? If you just stay angry and close off your heart so that no one can break it again, then you won't ever get your feelings hurt, right? If you take care of everyone around you and neglect your own physical, spiritual, and mental health, all of those people you love will love you even more because you are so selfless, right? Ask how that has worked out for me.

I know that my parents did their best when raising us. They didn't have the best parenting role models, and they didn't talk about their feelings or work through their childhood trauma. I am writing this on the first anniversary of my dad's unexpected passing in September of 2023. He told me many stories about his father's concept of "love."

Love was obedience. Love was respect, even when it wasn't earned. Love was a responsibility. And love was only given after achievement. My dad's family is from Venezuela. That is where he was born, the oldest of eight children. He loved his mom, Abuela. I think that he felt like he had to protect her from Abuelo. He watched over his younger siblings all his life. He believed it was his responsibility to provide for them and offer them guidance.

We were a lot alike, Dad and I, but most of those parts are the ones that I like least about myself. He was always striving to prove himself, to better himself, to make his life matter, to live up to someone else's standards (his father's). He did so many things wrong because he just didn't know better, but I believe that his steps were ordered, just like mine.

He always wanted to come to the United States. He was smart and knew he could make a better life for himself. He won a car in a raffle at a fair in Venezuela, which he sold to buy his ticket to freedom and wealth. He knew someone who lived in Louisiana, so he wrote a letter to them to alert them of his arrival and his need for a place to stay. This was the same letter that he retrieved from their mailbox upon arriving at their home to find them out of town. He was now in a country he knew very little about and where he didn't speak the language. He was finally able to reach his friends and stay at their house until they returned, but they were not prepared to house him long term. They supported him for a little while until he could apply and begin college, but he then needed to find somewhere else to stay.

He was resourceful, however, moving from friend's home to friend's home, couch surfing. He earned a place on their couch by cooking for them. College is also where he met my mom, whom he loved for the rest of his life. He just had an unhealthy way of expressing it, which resulted in years of family upset and upheaval, eventually ending in divorce. I used to pray that Mom would leave Dad, or wish that I just didn't have a dad. I thought it would be easier not to have one, rather than living in the constant state of fear that was my life. I am not sure that I even realized it was fear at the time— I didn't know how it would affect every aspect of my psychology and my adult life.

I know now that we hear and see information all the time, at least I do, because I work with children, about how much weight and impact your words can have. But, unless you are a product of hurtful words, you might not get it. Most people don't know, or don't try to understand, why they do or act a certain way. It takes deep digging into those parts of you that you have been suppressing or ignoring for so many years.

I would like to share some stories from my past so that we can examine how I perceived them, the long-term effects on my personality and overall personal development, and the lessons I've learned from them. Here's what I've learned: Don't give up yet; forgiveness is not only possible but crucial to your healing.

Forgiveness is where my shift truly started, the avenue I turned down that led to a more fulfilling life, and the doorway I flung open to abundance and living out my dreams.

I was left standing at the entrance of a neighborhood I didn't know while I watched him drive away. With tears streaming down my face, I wasn't sure how I was going to get home, nor could I tell if I was more afraid that he wouldn't come back or if he would. One thing felt certain: The feeling of relief from being out of the car was much greater than the fear of not getting home. This is the moment I realized a deep sense of helplessness. These feelings would stay with me well into adulthood and surfaced with a vengeance after we lost our first child.

You are probably wondering who "he" is, scenarios of kidnapping or an abusive boyfriend, maybe a husband. The man who left me standing in a strange part of town after holding me captive in a speeding car, driving erratically, nearly crashing more than once, and screaming wildly about problems that I didn't know anything about was my father. I don't remember exactly how old I was, but it was somewhere between ages eight and twelve. This whole tirade began because I did not meet his standards on the ball field. His standard was the only standard, and no one could tell him any different. He coached me in several sports: basketball, softball, soccer. To everyone looking in from the outside, he was an involved, invested, and supportive father.

On this particular day, I had played a softball game. By this stage of my life, my self-esteem or sense of self-worth was nonexistent. I didn't enjoy playing sports, but I didn't know that I had a choice not to. I did what my dad told me to do. I was a good girl. However, this girl was consumed by fear of everything. Dad was having a hard time finding a place for me to play on the ball field because I was afraid of being hit with the ball—probably because I had been. Second base was no good, shortstop wasn't a good fit, and third base is where I took a bounding line drive to the face.

We eventually settled on the outfield (which I was very good at, by the way), but this particular day, he thought the best way to cure me of my fear was to put me behind home plate. This is where not only is the ball coming at your face extremely often, but there is also an opponent swinging a bat every couple of minutes, barely missing your noggin. This is the perfect place for a kid who is scared of the ball. If you didn't read that last line with complete and total sarcasm, please reread it.

You can visualize how this played out. I was crying and begging to be moved from behind the plate; Mom stood at the fence several times to try to calm me and yelled at Dad to move me from behind the plate. Dad yelled at me and Mom in front of God and everyone.

I am fairly certain that is why he embarked on that terrifying ride after the game. We embarrassed him. We went against his wishes. I didn't learn the lesson he was trying to teach, and it made him look bad. I realize now that he was doing the best he could with the tools he had been given. He was trying to be supportive. He was trying to make me stronger. He was trying to make me brave, but in that moment, I had never felt less supported, weaker, or more scared in my entire life, both inside that car and at home every day.

Let me provide you with a bit more context.

My grandfather once taught my dad a lesson. When Dad was a kid, he wanted to play baseball with his friends after school. His dad told him to come straight home, and, like most kids testing their boundaries would, he opted to play baseball instead. I don't know whether or not there was an immediate punishment, but that might have worked out better for Dad. His father decided that it would be a better idea to punish him in the long term. He didn't buy Dad any shoes for an entire year. An entire year. This forced Dad to either wear shoes that were too small or too big, borrow used shoes from friends, or even cut the toes out to make more room for his growing feet. This year, without shoes, he caused permanent damage to his feet.

Most would agree that this was not a fitting punishment for wanting to have fun with your friends. The funny thing is (not funny "ha, ha") that growing up in a household like that must have meant my dad never felt safe, never felt heard, never felt seen, and may not have felt loved. As much as I hate to admit it, Dad and I were very much alike.

Writing this now, at forty-eight, I realize why I never felt safe. That feeling of being unsafe is not debilitating anymore, but I can be triggered pretty easily. One of my husband's least favorite things to do is ride with me in the car while he is driving. The sounds that come out of me, the jump scares, and my anxiety level tend to cause him anger. He always says that I am going to cause him to wreck for no good reason.

I've never told him the story of my dad leaving me in an unfamiliar neighborhood; I'm not sure I have ever told anyone this story. I guess the whole world will know now. They'll also know I'm not mad at Dad anymore.

This book contains many things that may shock you. Family members might feel guilty or be mad at me for sharing, but Dad isn't here anymore, and I plan to be around for a very long time. I must move through these memories and push past these old fears so that I can continue to grow and help others heal.

Before I was able to confront my past, I had been hearing the whisper of forgiveness for years and years. The word evoked an adverse physical reaction: recoil, an ache in my neck, tightness in my chest, and a pit in my stomach. My father didn't deserve to be forgiven, and I could prove it. I have story upon story of the verbal abuse and disregard for his family's emotions.

I will tell you that I did forgive him—two weeks before he passed. I do not regret forgiving him, but I do regret the timing. You may have heard this a thousand times, but forgiveness is not for the benefit of the other person. It is to allow love back into your own heart. Resentment, hate, anger, or whatever form your unforgiveness takes will grow roots and tangles that strangle your heart. It took me years to come to terms with the fact that it was up to me to apologize to myself for waiting so long to forgive instead of waiting for an apology from Dad.

Dad only ever apologized to me one time in my life that I remember. I will tell you that story later, but realize that he had much to apologize for. He jump-started my unhealthy relationship with food, along with a laundry list of other unhealthy relationships.

I was a picky kid, and my mom was a nutrition major in college, so dinners filled with liver, Brussels sprouts, and eggplant were not my jam. I spent many nights sitting in front of a full plate of food for hours because I wasn't allowed to leave the table until I had cleared my plate. If you cannot already imagine the psychological damage that this can cause, let me explain.

Although I did not want to eat some of the healthy foods my mom cooked, the seed of "clear your plate" was planted. I began to dig my heels in at the dinner table, but still felt like I had no control over most aspects of my life. Instead of eating food at the family dinner table, I began to hide my eating.

I distinctly remember pulling day-old Captain D's fish out of my sister's trash can and eating it where no one could see me. Who does that? I never considered myself to have an eating disorder because I never purged, but I certainly binged, cycling through long periods of not eating. Sometimes, I would eat when no one was around, much like my dad used to eat ice cream at 3 a.m. If no one was there to see me eat, did I really eat at all?

Every challenge or problem I have faced, including trauma and grief, I've been able to move through and persevere by first educating myself. I needed to better understand trauma—the different types, the differences and similarities in how people reacted to it, that I wasn't the only one who had experienced it, how it could affect my physical body, that I could work through it, and that it wasn't my fault.

I needed to better understand grief and how it was affecting relationships in my life, why it was causing mental health issues, that we can grieve more than death, that there is no right or wrong way to grieve, and that it looks different for every person.

I needed to understand how it could consume my every thought and action, and that ignoring moving through it could cause me to live on autopilot.

I needed to research the very rare gene that my husband and I carried that turned our dreams into nightmares.

I needed to better educate myself on how Dad's childhood affected his ability to parent me so that I could extend forgiveness.

I sought a postgraduate degree to gain a deeper understanding of my son's brain, the way he perceives the world, and how he processes sensory information, so that I could be a more effective parent to him.

I needed to have a better understanding of bone cancer to prepare myself for the possibility that my leg may be amputated.

I embarked on a journey of self-care and self-healing because if I did not truly love myself or know how to process my feelings, how could I be everything my family and friends needed me to be?

I wish I had thought of the E.A.T. concept much earlier in my life. It could have saved me years of suffering in silence and feeling like I was so alone. We will dive deep into this framework in Chapter 12, but let me give you a thousand-foot view for now. Because I spent nearly four decades eating my feelings instead of digesting life's truths, I decided to turn the pattern that almost killed me upside down to heal me.

Trauma-Anxiety-Eat (T.A.E.) slowly became Educate-Accept-Transform (E.A.T.). My patterns of stuffing down trauma after trauma built my levels of anxiety higher and higher, fueling my unhealthy coping mechanism of eating instead of processing what I was truly feeling. Now, when trauma or life's challenges happen—and they will happen—I first *educate* myself on the problem at hand. That will look different for different situations. I then *accept* the parts of the challenge that I cannot control or change in that moment (or perhaps ever). Those parts are too big for me to handle, and I will give them to God. The last step may take longer than the first two, and that is to *transform* those challenges into something positive, either to find a solution or to use my pain for someone else's progress in their journey.

I always say that I don't remember my childhood, which isn't entirely true. I remember some of it, and most of what I remember, I would like to forget.

My dad was complex, as you may have realized by now. However, I mostly remember him as being mean and unreasonable. I was such a shy kid and afraid to do or try most things. I would rather get lost in the imaginary world of a book than live in the real world. Everything outside of my bedroom seemed so foreign to me, and I never felt like I fit in, especially in my own home. I think I stayed in my room to avoid contact with my father. He was always yelling about something or yelling at someone.

Out of sight, out of mind, right? If he didn't see me, he wouldn't scream at me. I remember being afraid of almost everything then. I can't pinpoint when that started, but nearly everything gave me that sunken pit-in-your-stomach feeling, except food. Food was my friend.

Horse pills, on the other hand, were not. I was sick a lot as a kid, with terrible sinus issues. Dad smoked when we were younger, so I have always blamed it on him. I would get terrible sinus infections that would keep me down for a week or more at a time.

I was on antibiotics quite often, which also may have something to do with the gut imbalance I experience now, but more on that later. Once I got "old enough"—somewhere between eight and ten years old—to swallow a pill, the doctor stopped prescribing liquid antibiotics. I *could not* swallow that pill. Mom worked with me, and I tried. I knew the formula: Put the pill on the back of your tongue, take a big swig of liquid, throw your head back like a maniac laughing at their diabolical plan, and swallow the dang pill. I just couldn't do it, no matter how many times I tried. It would become all wet, soggy, and bitter-tasting, and I would just roll it around in there until it dissolved. Got the job done, right? Not according to my father.

He happened to walk in during one of my pill-swallowing battles. He was appalled that I was having so much trouble swallowing a pill. How could I be so stupid? What was wrong with me? If I had trouble doing something so simple, how could I ever make it in life? What he failed to realize is that I was afraid to swallow the pill. My anxiety was so out of control at eight, nine, ten years old that I was certain if I swallowed that pill whole, it would be lodged in my throat, no one would know how to do the Heimlich, and I would slowly suffocate there on my kitchen floor while my dad yelled at me because I couldn't even die correctly.

It's no wonder that I had no self-esteem as a kid. I'm sure that Mom gave me words of encouragement, but I don't remember. I remember my room, I remember my bed, and I remember the built-in dresser unit on my bedroom wall. I remember my bathroom and my older sister's bedroom, which was right next to ours (my little sister and I shared a room). If I close my eyes, I can take a tour of that entire house, room by room, but I don't see myself there. I don't see my family there. I don't feel any sensations in my body about that house one way or the other, except for relief. I am relieved that I no longer live there. I'm grateful for the roof over my head and all the nice things, but as I remember that house, it just feels like an empty shell. That is how I often felt.

I have always felt out of place, out of sorts, and like I was an outsider in every situation. This year, 2024, is the first year that the skin I am in is mine. I feel confident, intelligent, and capable of pursuing my dreams. This did not happen overnight, and from the glimpse that I have given you into my childhood so far, you know that I didn't leave that house with tools, strategies, or any kind of coping skills to help me navigate the outside world. Sometimes I wonder how I managed to get this far. God's grace is the only possible explanation. He knew all along what I was capable of and how I could impact other people's lives.

I used to think that I was surviving simply by coasting on autopilot, which was true for some of my journey. Still, I was using mental strategies, physical strategies, and spiritual strategies along the way without even knowing it. I was implementing the E.A.T. framework before it was fully developed. Part of the reason that I decided to title this book *Eat Your Feelings* is because that was the most prevalent unhealthy coping mechanism I was using at the time, and the one that most people refer to when speaking about stressful situations. Eating my feelings instead of digesting the truth surrounding painful situations. We often say it in passing or in a joking tone because we don't want to acknowledge it for what it is: avoidance.

Even writing this makes me want to eat chocolate and something crunchy and salty. The devil knows that food is one of my most significant weaknesses, and he uses it as often as he can to distract me from what God has planned. The problem with food addiction is that we need food to live. I never turned to alcohol (I've had alcohol less than twenty times in my entire life). I didn't turn to drugs. I don't like feeling out of control. Did you catch that? I want to be in control of my thoughts, actions, and body. So, the very thing that tormented me as a child saved me from becoming a drug addict or an alcoholic—but I did become addicted to food. I know I was addicted because I would hide it. I still hide it sometimes.

Even when I actively tried to change my lifestyle, I still didn't feel like I fit in. Everyone (or what I perceived to be everyone) would make fun of me or try to get me to eat things I shouldn't be eating. I have had many people do this with alcohol as well. I don't judge others for what they eat or drink, so stop judging me. I will no longer apologize for trying to keep myself alive. I was slowly killing myself by eating my feelings. All of the feelings, all of the shame, all of the guilt that I stuffed down deep into my soul have begun leaking out and poisoning my system and my health.

My digestive system, my skeletal system, my nervous system, my mental health, my physical health, my spiritual health. There is no magic pill (even though I am currently taking over twenty-five different supplements). No one thing will magically fix all of your problems.

I have spent years working on my relationship with God. I have spent years working on my marriage. I have spent years working on healing my body. I have spent years processing the trauma I was subjected to as a child. I have spent years feeling lonely, unseen, and unheard. I have spent years always feeling left out. Don't be like the old me. Start to reframe the way you look at your challenges so they don't feel like such a big pill to swallow. Perspective is everything, and if I have learned nothing else, I have learned that perspective can also change everything.

CHAPTER 2
MARRIAGE
(HOT HONEY BARBECUE WINGS)

"He's short, *and* his name is Donald?"

This was my first reaction to the man my sister suggested I meet: Strike one and strike two.

"Well, he kinda looks like your ex-boyfriend a little bit."

This was strike number three. I didn't want to date anything or anybody remotely resembling my ex-boyfriend. He doesn't look anything like my ex-boyfriend, by the way. They both have blue eyes, but that's the only thing they have in common. I told my sister that he didn't sound like anyone I wanted to date, but he had seen my picture and was interested in me, so I agreed to talk with him by phone.

That's how the whole thing started. We spoke on the phone for about three weeks, and looking back now, I can say that I was in love with him before I ever saw him. It wouldn't have mattered if he looked like Quasimodo and climbed down from a bell tower. I was already in love with him by the time we met in person. I also found out that his friends and family called him Donnie, not Donald. The deal was sealed.

Through our phone conversations, I discovered that Donnie had been living in Tennessee for almost five years at the time. His sister was killed in a car accident when she was sixteen and he was eighteen, which was in 1994. His mom just couldn't live in the place where they had lived for so many years. Everywhere she looked, she saw her daughter, and she needed to get away. My husband went with her. His parents bought property in Tennessee, but his dad stayed in Florida because he had a long-time job there. For several years, they met in Georgia, and several times a year, his dad would drive to Tennessee to be with his mom. They stayed together the entire time, which is incredible after losing their sixteen-year-old daughter in a car accident, an accident where they never found out what exactly happened.

But theirs was the example of marriage that my husband was fortunate enough to see. His parents have been married for over fifty-five years, and they still look at each other as if they had just started dating. My example of marriage was less endearing. I suppose that I was fortunate enough to learn firsthand what I didn't want in a marriage. I didn't marry a man like my father, but I did take on his most undesirable traits for most of my life. Changing those patterns has been painful, challenging, and worth every minute. As we all know, or should know, unhealed wounds only fester and slowly kill you from the inside out.

Donnie has never honestly dealt with the death of his sister. We have a lot in common, and one of those things is stuffing down our feelings. When you go through a lot of trauma, your sense of humor gets a little bit warped. We often joke that he is dead inside. I have always said that he has a little box where he puts all the bad things and then closes the lid—forever. That worked for him for a little while, years. But my question to him often these days is, "How is that working out for ya?"

He recently reached out to a counselor. I am proud of him for taking that step, and we are hopeful that it will help him let go of the past that he couldn't control.

The near downfall in our marriage is that we forgot to communicate with each other. I don't recommend not communicating with your spouse, but I'll discuss that more later. He was living in Tennessee when we met. He worked with my older sister at a sign company. He had a long-time girlfriend who started talking about marriage, but she was the only one who mentioned it. He broke up with her, but was also moping around the office. His mom had just recently moved back to Florida, and he was girlfriendless when my older sister said, "Hey, I have a younger sister not seeing anybody right now."

She showed him my picture, and she set us up on a kind of blind date. She gave me his phone number and gave him my phone number. I don't remember who called who first, but our schedules were very busy at the time. He was working full-time and going to college, and I was a full-time college student. We started talking in 1998, so I had to have been at least a junior and was nearing the end of my college career. He barely had time to sleep or eat, much less do anything else. So we talked on the phone for about three weeks before we ever saw each other.

The first time Donnie wanted me to meet his parents was going to be on the anniversary of his sister's death. They were also going to a monster truck rally. I love monster trucks now, but back then, it wasn't my thing. There were no parts of that scenario that seemed conducive to a successful first date.

When we first met face-to-face, I finally understood the age-old saying, "When you know, you know." You can't understand what that means until you meet the person that you're supposed to spend the rest of your life with. I just knew.

I'm going to date myself here, but our first date was to see the movie *Titanic* at the movie theater. Afterward, we went to dinner at a local restaurant, which had some of the best chicken fingers, or chicken "sticks," as we liked to call them, that you could ever eat. We then went to Baskin-Robbins for ice cream. At this point in my life, I was very gassy, but did not realize that I was lactose intolerant. So, ice cream for dessert after popcorn at the movie, and then chicken sticks with white gravy, along with French fries and bread, were not healthy choices for me.

That's what we ate back then because we didn't know any better. We didn't know what to eat that was good for our bodies or how to process our compounding trauma that we were both bringing into the relationship. But at this point, ignorance was bliss. After the movie, popcorn, dinner, and ice cream, we were in the truck on the way back to my dorm. As I was talking, all of a sudden, I burped—mid-sentence, right in his face. I wanted to open the door, roll out of the truck, and just die from mortification right there on the side of the road.

But Donnie said, "Oh! Now we're getting to know each other!"

It was probably at that moment that he knew that he wanted to marry me, too.

Our relationship progressed quickly from there. We were engaged within three months of meeting each other and married within a year. We decided to get married on the anniversary of his sister's death to honor her. We felt like she was there with us that day. There were snow flurries right about the time the wedding was to begin. It made it a happy date, not just a sad one, for his family.

As I said before, he had never truly processed his sister's death. He and his mom left Florida after she died. Like a lot of people do when they grieve, I, being one of them, run. You try to run from your fear, your trauma, your grief. But the problem with running is that no matter where you run, *you* are still there. You can't run from yourself. So you have to move through these things, which I did not learn easily or quickly.

Don't think I'm judging if you are currently running. I did it for years, and he's still doing it.

But in the beginning, we were happy. We moved to Florida because he was now an only child, and his parents wanted to be close to him. His mom had moved back the year before, and they offered for us to live in his grandmother's old house.

Newly married with a free house? yes please. He had a job, but I did not because I had just graduated from college. We barely had two cents to rub together. He had saved a little bit, but I don't remember having anything, because I had learned to spend money, like my dad did, rather than save it.

We started in a two-bedroom, one-bath concrete block home. I loved that house, with its drop-down ceilings, window air conditioning units, and no shortage of roaches. None of that mattered because it was ours. It was our house, so I loved it. I loved Donnie. I loved wherever he was, and we were happy.

I ended up getting a job, my first job. I had a four-year degree in biology, which will be important later, but that first job didn't care what my degree was in. They just liked that I had a degree. I got that job because when we went to buy a television for our "new to us" house with no money, we needed to purchase it on credit. So, we took out a loan, which in those days was similar to a credit card, but it was more of a formal contract. When the manager of the financial company called to verify our application, she offered me a job. Linda, who I'm still friends with today and currently coach in my fitness and nutrition program, hired me over the phone. For that, I will be forever grateful.

After that job, I went into banking. Donnie was working in Orlando when we first got married, but he soon landed a job building homes for The Villages, where he still works now, more than twenty-five years later.

We had fun in our first few years of marriage, or at least I think we did, but I just don't remember. Another reason for me to write this book is to bring more memories to the surface. I'm sure I have forgotten things because they were painful. But I do remember being happy.

My dad and I did not have a good relationship at that point, and he proceeded to tell my husband that all he would ever be was a maintenance man because he didn't have a four-year degree. The bottom line of that conversation was that nobody was good enough for his little girl, but my dad didn't know how to express those kinds of feelings. All he knew was how to put others down to make his point, and that is how he spoke to my husband. My husband didn't appreciate this exchange, but we had moved away from my family for a reason.

We were happy even though we lived paycheck to paycheck—and beyond our means. We weren't saving money. We were young when we got married. I was twenty-two, and he was twenty-three. We were kids learning as we went.

A few years into our marriage, I was late for my period. We hadn't talked about getting pregnant up to this point. It wasn't that we didn't want to—we just hadn't talked about it. Can you see a theme with communication?

So, I got it in my head that I was pregnant, and I was thrilled. I went to the doctor, and I was *not* pregnant. Of course, I decided that we should start trying. We got pregnant pretty quickly, and my husband's cousin got pregnant about a month after I did.

Everyone was overjoyed that the daughters were pregnant at the same time. We were shopping for maternity clothes and nursery bedding, and doing all the things that you do when you're elated to be having a baby. We'll get into the pregnancy in a later chapter; just know that the elation would not last.

My husband and I both carry a very rare gene that makes very sick babies. My husband has never fully processed the death of his sister, so when we went to that ultrasound where we found out something was wrong, he left the room and went out to the sidewalk, where he sat down and cried. I believe that's the last time that he ever cried. He detached right then and there. He detached from the situation, detached from the pregnancy, and detached from me, because he didn't have the coping strategies he needed to process the current situation that we were facing.

He put all those things in that little box that he carries in the back of his mind, but even detached, he supported me. He knew how to do that. When he came back into the hospital after that ultrasound, he supported me. At the specialty hospital, when they told us that our baby had a lethal condition, he supported me. He supported me the best way he knew how. He held my hand, he kissed me on the cheek, and he held me when I cried.

When we went to the hospital after my water broke, he was there the entire time, holding my hand, screaming in my face to breathe when I was in the most challenging part of my labor. He was there to hold our daughter after she was born. He always wants to fix the problem. He always wants to make it better.

But some things you can't make better. He couldn't fix that situation, and he couldn't fix me. He hated to see me cry, and I couldn't talk about anything without crying. I learned that he didn't want to see me cry, and he learned that if I didn't talk about anything, then I didn't cry. So that's what we did. We stopped talking about everything. We worked and we paid the bills, and we hid things from each other. None of these things work—in a marriage or in life.

We really love each other, especially now that we've been through everything we've been through. I can tell you that we really love each other. We are best friends, we are business partners, we are parents. Our life has been hard, and I couldn't help him with his grief because I was just trying to keep myself alive.

You will be happy to hear that we did adopt, and you'll find out more about that later as well. Adoption was also very stressful, and we incurred a great deal of credit card debt, through a little retail therapy as well as adoption expenses. When we finally received the babies we had prayed for so fervently, suddenly, it was all about them.

There wasn't much time for communication, there wasn't time for date night, there wasn't time to go on vacation, and there wasn't time to talk to one another. When we did speak to each other, we fought about money, learning quickly that it was yet another area where we weren't able to communicate.

He hated to talk about money because we never had enough. I started to take care of paying all the bills, which created another heightened state of anxiety for me—I was robbing Peter to pay Paul, as they say. You can get pretty crafty transferring balances to pay off another credit card. I just started not talking to him about it, while I was transferring money from savings to cover overdrafts. I didn't want to upset him or fight, so I just took all of the responsibility on myself. I wasn't very good at asking for help in the past, but I'm changing that pattern now.

One day, I don't remember the year, I noticed he had lost a lot of weight, and he was very concerned with his appearance. Suddenly, he was very worried about me knowing his whereabouts—and making sure I couldn't see his phone.

I should have seen the signs.

I knew there were signs, but I chose to ignore them because that's what I did at that time. I ignored all the things that made me sad or that I didn't want to deal with. Instead, I filled the void with food, and instead of truly digesting them, I just ate my feelings. Perhaps if you simply ignore all the bad things, they will magically disappear. That doesn't work; I strongly recommend an alternative plan.

We had started to take our health more seriously and were dabbling in self-development. I had been selling Avon for a number of years, and we joined a health and wellness multi-level marketing company together. We attended conferences where motivational or inspirational speakers told stories of healing and wealth generation through direct selling.

This marked the beginning of prioritizing my health and our marriage. I had gained a significant amount of weight by this point.

There was also quite a bit of yo-yo weight happening because I had never really lost the weight from the babies, and then the doctors put me on antidepressants. Obviously, I was depressed because I had experienced massive losses.

You will learn more about these in later chapters, but we didn't lose just one child. I miscarried soon after our first child was born, and then we cremated two more infants. But all those antidepressant drugs did was make me puffy. I had no idea how to eat healthfully or what to eat to be healthier, so I just kept putting on weight, feeling bad about myself, and causing more depression. Sex was obviously not on my radar, but it is always on my husband's. This is probably not new news to you, but many men need physical touch, and they are very visual creatures. This created a perfect storm for marital problems.

One evening, back in the days when Facebook was relatively new, I got up to go to the bathroom in the middle of the night. Donnie's phone was on the bathroom counter, and it lit up as I walked by. It's probably not a coincidence. What we do in the dark is always brought into the light.

The DM read, *"Are you up?"*

And I thought, another woman should not be messaging my husband in the middle of the night, asking him if he's up.

I woke him up right then and there, "What is this? What does this mean? Why is she messaging you?" He didn't truly deny it, but claimed that he didn't know. He didn't know how to use Facebook. He didn't think you could use Messenger.

What you need to understand is that this woman was not a stranger. This was someone with whom he had a long-term relationship, previous to me. Someone who he had been very close to, his first love. I found out years later that she said all the right things. She offered him everything he thought he wanted. She looked the right way. She was very thin, with beautiful, long hair. She listened to him, and she told him what he needed to hear. I certainly was not doing any of those things. Even though I wasn't very forgiving after I found out, I don't blame anyone anymore.

Neither one of them was happy. She knew exactly what she was doing, thinking she knew what she wanted at the time. He was feeling inadequate as a man, as a husband, as a father. All I wanted was a baby, and he couldn't give that to me. We probably could have had sex with any other person in the city, in the state, maybe even in the country, and had a healthy baby. I think, perhaps he thought, well, if she leaves me, then she could have a baby with somebody else.

I'm getting a little ahead of myself, though, here. After seeing that DM and hearing his denials, I let it go because he stopped with the "weird" for a little while. He regained the weight he had lost. He stopped sneaking around, and we went back to being stressed about the kids and not having any money. But he eventually started acting strange again. He started saying bizarre things like, "If we ever get divorced, you can't take the kids away from me," or "If you ever leave me, you can't keep me from seeing the kids."

I thought, *Why is he saying these weird things? Did I say I was leaving him?* I didn't understand. I still had my head in the sand about a lot of things. I was still walking around like a zombie in a fog most days, and the cheating had never been confirmed nor denied.

Then, I came down with strep throat and a 102-degree fever. I could barely pick my head up off the pillow. My throat felt like razor blades mixed with broken glass every time I swallowed. All I could do was cry. On the second day that I had strep throat, I started my period. I was utterly miserable. My husband was acting manic on this particular day. He was cleaning everything in the house. He was cleaning all the vehicles. He was pacing and asking me way too often if I needed anything. He finally sat down on the couch next to my recliner. He was wringing his hands and then got up to pace back and forth.

That's when it came out. He said, "I need to tell you something." I couldn't even talk, literally, because of my strep throat. At this point, I was a captive audience because I couldn't move and couldn't speak.

He told me that he cheated on me and started rambling on about telling the kids and his parents. He wanted to tell whoever I thought he should tell. I didn't make him do any of that, of course, I'm telling the whole world now, but at that time, I just needed time to process what had happened. I wasn't mad, I wasn't even sad, I was just deeply disappointed. I had told him long ago that there were a lot of things that I would tolerate, but cheating wasn't one of them. I had been cheated on before, and I had promised myself that I would never let anyone disrespect me like that again.

But God convinced him to tell me because He wanted our relationship to be renewed. Sometimes, the very thing that is meant to break you is precisely what you need to have a breakthrough.

The moment that he told me he cheated was the beginning of taking care of myself. In that instant, I realized that I couldn't give him what he needed until I started loving myself again. This began our journey of health and wellness; it started my journey of fitness, self-development, and a desire to better communicate with others.

This marked the beginning of my understanding that educating myself on the challenges I was facing would help me accept what I could not control. I wanted to learn how to transform that pain into something that could make a difference, not only for me and my family but for others. I have said—all these years later—that I'm glad he cheated on me. Because if he hadn't, I may have never changed my life. That was the wake-up call I needed. It was the wake-up call he needed. He knew that he wasn't living his life the way he was supposed to be living it. From that point forward, we did everything as a team. We never do anything without discussing it with one another. We never make decisions without consulting each other. We are not perfect at discussing money, but we do so in a more open manner now than we ever have before.

We started going to church. We serve together in the church and have formed long-lasting friendships through the life groups we've been a part of. Marriage can be very sweet, but it can also be spicy, and the heat from transgressions and mistakes can linger like the fire from hot honey barbeque wings. It is also hard, and it is up to both sides to work at it. And in all of that, you have to take care of yourself first. You have to pour into yourself before you can fully love anyone else, especially your family, the way they deserve to be loved.

CHAPTER 3
KAELYNN ALECIA, MARCH 26– 29, 2002
(STRAWBERRY SHORTCAKE)

I don't see anything, but I feel someone holding my hand. It takes me a few minutes to remember where I am. This hospital room is dark and small, but I can hear the muffled noises and voices outside the door. I keep staring at my hand. I can't see through my sleepy, tear-swollen eyes. I feel someone holding my hand, and then the waking nightmare that I am currently starring in comes rushing back to me. I feel it is Abuela holding my hand. I can almost see her face smiling at me, her eyes saying everything will be okay.

Abuela is there to comfort me as my worst nightmare has come true. She was born earlier today, our first child and the first grandchild on both sides of the family. She is beautifully broken and perfectly formed by God's hand. I just can't figure out why she can't stay. Why has this happened to us? What did we do?

I don't remember discussing having children when my husband and I started dating. I knew that I had always loved children and wanted to have babies. I have always been fascinated with the human body and was elated about the idea of a tiny person growing inside of me. I was excited, but surprisingly uneasy for some reason. I couldn't put my finger on why and never said anything to anyone, but I felt like something was going to be wrong even before I ever got pregnant.

I have always had "a feeling" about things. Little decisions, big decisions, events, happenings—I go with my gut, or I push that "feeling" down inside. I forge ahead anyway.

I used to think that I was weak-minded and not quite good enough at anything that I had ever done, but this is what I knew I wanted. This, I knew, was going to be beautiful. This, I knew, was supposed to happen. I would have a beautiful baby with my curly hair and Donnie's almond-shaped, brilliant blue eyes. I would do everything right. I never smoked, didn't do drugs, and was always the designated driver in college. I took my prenatal vitamins, went to pregnant yoga, and played music for the baby while she was inside my womb. I had such a fairytale expectation of the entire process, but I should have listened to that "feeling" a little more carefully. Our experience was anything but a fairytale.

I told you the story earlier about being late one month to my cycle and then deciding to get pregnant. What I didn't tell you is that my period had never been late before. My body was a well-oiled period-producing machine. Even daylight saving time didn't throw it off. So when I was late, I just knew that I was pregnant. But the pee stick said otherwise, and the doctor said otherwise, so I forged ahead and declared that this must be a sign. I'm big on signs; I see them everywhere, in everything, but more on that later.

It was a sign. We were supposed to start trying to get pregnant, and no sooner had the words escaped my lips—I was pregnant. This is our curse. We can look at each other and get pregnant. It was a glorious time, so innocent and happy. My booty got wide, my belly grew, and at about four or five months, we had a routine ultrasound where they measure this and that and tell you the sex... *yada yada yada*.

I can still hear the doctor's voice on the answering machine: "The baby's limbs are measuring a little short for this stage in your pregnancy, but you and Donnie aren't tall people, so it's nothing to worry about right now"—or something to that effect.

Donnie's first reaction was, "I don't want a dwarf baby," and I replied by saying that dwarves were cute, and I would love to have his dwarf baby, which I did about twelve weeks later.

We found out something was deeply wrong at my six-month check-up. The nurse commented on how much my belly had grown in such a short period. I didn't have any idea how big my belly was supposed to be. Maybe it's trying to keep up with my butt, because it was rather large. And then the doctor was very quiet while measuring my belly, mumbling something about not being able to find my fundus. When he started the ultrasound and proclaimed that I had too much amniotic fluid, tears immediately began to roll down my cheeks. I didn't know what that meant, but I had that feeling again, and it wasn't a good one.

Over the next several weeks, we embarked on a journey of doctor's appointments with ultrasound after ultrasound, one of which brought our entire world crashing down.

Both of our parents were present in that tiny room at the specialty women's hospital when the doctor arrived.

As she said, "This is a lethal condition," it was like the room was suddenly under water. There was so much pressure on my body, and I couldn't breathe. Someone screamed out, but it sounded so far away. Was it me screaming? Was it in my head, or was it out loud? I'm still not sure.

At the time, I wasn't sure of anything except that my baby girl was going to die. I only heard part of what the doctor said. Still, I remember her saying that they didn't think that she would even survive the birthing process, so this very active, tiny soul inside my womb who kicked me every single day would not and could not thrive outside of the safe place that I now provided her.

I thought to myself, *I am so sorry, baby girl. None of this is your fault, and I would take your suffering in a quick minute if God would allow it.*

After the crying and wailing subsided, I know that my Mom asked some brilliant and needed questions, but I don't remember them or any of the answers. I only remember going home and staying pregnant for about a month and a half with my precious baby, who had been given a death sentence. I didn't want to leave the house or talk to anyone. I just tried to breathe in and out and have faith, and I clung to the hope that maybe they were wrong. This was my baby, and she would surprise all of them because she had a strong heart, and God couldn't possibly take her from me.

We had to make funeral arrangements, which was devastating. We made an appointment at the cemetery and rendered the man speechless after he asked who the arrangements were for, and I simply placed my hand on my swollen belly. My husband's sister, Christie, had already been laid to rest in this very cemetery.

Losing a child is not for the faint of heart; this task is given to God's true warriors. You see, my name, Cristina, means "follower of Christ," and my mother-in-law's name, Sandra, means "defender of mankind." That's why my mother-in-law and I were born warriors for Jesus.

My momma, Rebecca Susan—whose name means "woman of charming beauty and graceful lily"—was able to stay strong and hold it all together, asking questions at the hospital about what to expect and what would come next.

But at the cemetery, when the funeral director started talking about burying our daughter at the head of the grave so that I could join her when I passed, my beautiful momma disappeared into the cemetery, and we couldn't find her for a time. All of this was too much to process, but I think that it comforted us to know that Aunt Christie and her niece would be side by side. We decided to name the baby Kaelynn. I loved "K" names for some reason, and we wanted to use Lynn because that was Christie's middle name.

I started to avoid going out because innocent strangers asked me so many questions. How far along are you? When are you due? What are you having?

I was screaming inside my head: *"I'M HAVING A DEAD BABY GIRL, PROBABLY ANY MINUTE, STAND BACK SO YOU DON'T GET DEATH SPLASHED ON YOU!"*

It was hard to smile and answer and not cry. My focus became getting through each day, and this continued until March 26, 2002. That was the day my water broke because the amniotic fluid was too much for my uterus to hold. I heard a popping sound, like a water balloon being hurled at a brick wall, and Niagara Falls came gushing out. Not exaggerating here, I wobbled to the bathroom and got in the tub as fast as I could, where the fluid just kept coming out.

I called my mother-in-law, who sent my father-in-law because he was the closest to me, but before hanging up with her, I asked, "Do I have to put on pants?"

We were heading to the doctor's office, where they needed to confirm that my water had broken. I was sure the ten pounds of fluid that just erupted from my nether region was my water breaking, but we humored them. So, we called my Donnie, who had parked the car far from his office, which meant he had to make a full-on sprint of about three-quarters of a mile just to get to the car. Yes, I put on pants, sat on a towel in the car, and off we went to the doctor, where they indeed determined that my water had broken.

I didn't want to go to the hospital in Orlando by ambulance. I had assumed I was in labor earlier that month and rode on a very hard gurney in the back of a very bumpy ambulance with very real and painful contractions for an hour. So now we drove ourselves there, and I stared at the outline of my baby still inside my much smaller abdomen all the way there. She was active even at that point. I often tormented myself, both while I was still pregnant and years in the future, by wondering if she moved so much because she was in pain. They told me that the reason I was filling with fluid was because she was able to excrete the liquid but not able to swallow any due to her tiny rib cage, which would be her undoing.

I was progressing very quickly through the birthing process. I was trying to fill out papers and sign documents while in the middle of full-on contractions, still leaking precious fluids, and in a fog about what was taking place. They put me on a gurney in a tiny room and said that they would move me when it was closer to delivery time.

Well, when I started white-knuckling the bed rail and quit breathing due to the pain, my husband got worried and called the nurse. I was eight centimeters dilated, and by the time they got me up two floors on the elevator and into the delivery room, tiny baby legs were hanging from my vagina. She was breech, which meant they had to do an epidural in case I needed an emergency c-section. It was all a whirlwind of chaos, me lying on my side with half a baby dangling between my legs. Someone explained the dangers and side effects of an epidural to me as the anesthesiologist was placing it in my back. My eyes were tightly shut, but I heard and felt all of the doctors and nurses around me, as well as my husband, who startled me by shouting in my face: "Breathe!"

I must have stopped breathing or was holding my breath, and then the next thing you know, they were pulling Kaelynn from me and rushing her over to a table nearby. I didn't hear any cries from her, she never cried, and I remember thinking that must mean she didn't make it.

Then I heard one of the nurses say, "Hey baby girl, there you are."

She made it, and when they brought her over so I could see her, all I could think was that she looked like my baby sister, Linnea. She was beautiful, and she had made it.

The following hours consisted of bringing in our parents to see her in case she passed because they expected her to leave us any minute. Remember back in Chapter 1 when I told you that Dad only ever apologized to me once in my life? This was that time.

I remember him sitting next to the hospital bed while I had Kaelynn in my arms. He cried as he stared at her and told me that he felt like this was all his fault. He was so sorry that I was being punished for his sins. My dad was raised Catholic, and although we never attended Catholic church or lived a Catholic lifestyle, you never saw him without his cross hanging around his neck. I still have his wall cross with Jesus nailed to it that he had hanging in every home he ever lived in.

One of the only scriptures he knew was Exodus 20:5, *"I, the Lord your God, am a jealous God, punishing children for the iniquity of parents, to the third and fourth generation of those who reject me."*

If he had studied the Bible more, he may have also found Ezekiel 18:20: *"The one who sins is the one who will die. The child will not share the guilt of the parent, nor will the parent share the guilt of the child. The righteousness of the righteous will be credited to them, and the wickedness of the wicked will be charged against them."*

The real lesson in both of these scriptures is to learn from the mistakes of those who have lived before us. Dad struggled with this his entire life, and I'm so sad that he didn't find more joy when he was alive. But I have used his mistakes as lessons in my life, and for that, I thank him. He was able to spend some time with his grandbaby, and I got a much-needed apology, though it didn't carry as much weight in that moment as it should have because I was in such a state of grief.

I was assigned a room near the nurse's station, and Kaelynn was placed in the NICU. I was the mom who didn't have the option of her baby sleeping in our room; we had to visit her, and the hours were limited.

Donnie and I had discussed that we didn't want to be there when she took her final breath. It almost took mine, having to sign the DNR for my daughter. I instructed very qualified and willing hospital personnel *not* to resuscitate my newborn child. Who does that? Why was I put in that position? When was this nightmare going to end?

We were all able to hold her and be with her over the next few days, but every time I held her in the NICU, the buzzers, flashers, and warnings would sound as her vital signs declined. I would hand her over to one of the grandmothers and run out of the room, waiting to hear that she was gone, but it never happened. Her vital signs would stabilize, and the nightmare continued.

The evening of March 28, I didn't sleep very well. I knew that she would die the next day. I had one of my feelings. There was a horrible, crushing weight sitting on my chest, and it was almost impossible to breathe. I felt my heart break into a million pieces that night—one tiny piece of which would never be found, because she would take it with her the next morning on the wings of Heaven.

God let me know that night that she was waiting for me to hold her when Jesus was on His way. I was her momma and could comfort her like no one else could. What an honor and a gift to be *that* important to someone else. She only needed and wanted me. I was the only home she had ever known, her safe place in this world.

We changed our minds about being with Kaelynn when she passed, and we were all gathered around when she took her final breath. I held her as everyone surrounded me, offering their support. It wasn't horrible at all; it was peaceful and quick. Just like that, she was gone to sit on the lap of Jesus, my own personal Angel. How did I get so lucky?

I realize what a blessing it is to become pregnant and have a healthy baby. I have several friends who were never able to become pregnant, let alone experience the miracle of labor and childbirth. I do consider myself quite blessed, but the experience left me broken: I still wince when I hear someone has found out that they are pregnant or when someone posts on Facebook that they are going into labor.

Many people don't realize the series of miraculous events that have to occur to carry fertilization to delivery. It truly is a miracle straight from Heaven, and I'm grateful for the fleeting moments I enjoyed on my journey to motherhood. For you see, it all started with my Kaelynn, but she was only the beginning of a long journey to our children here on earth. They are angels sent to us from God's adoption list, but their stories come much later in the journey. First, I need to tell you about laying our precious baby to rest.

I don't remember a great deal about the day of the funeral, to be quite honest. I remember the viewing and how my sweet husband warned me that she may not look like herself.

"They never get the lips quite right and try not to cry on her, the makeup will run," he said.

This was unfortunate knowledge that he learned from his sister's funeral years before.

Kaelynn was still beautiful in the miniature coffin that swallowed her tiny body. I wasn't sure that I wanted others to see all of her. Not that I was ashamed of what we had created, but I didn't want them to think poorly of her.

The gene that we carry that made her unwell causes Ellis-Van Creveld Syndrome. It is a musculoskeletal condition, and one of the symptoms is dwarfism. Her tiny limbs were the cutest, but she also had six fingers and six toes, a cleft palate, an enlarged head, a brain fissure that resulted in severe brain damage, a lethally sized rib cage, and several other health problems, according to the autopsy. Her heart was strong, though; she inherited that from her momma, and I am convinced that is why she was able to spend more time with us than the doctors had originally surmised. Never underestimate a *Simmons*—they are overcomers.

When we got the original diagnosis from the ultrasound and after enduring a very draining amniocentesis (please excuse my warped humor), I had visions of a very malformed fetus that I so lovingly carried. I wasn't sure if I would even be able to lay eyes on her when she was born.

Could I love a disfigured child? What would everyone else think?

Had our love created a monster? Would our love monster hate us for being born? Was she in pain all of the time? Would she know that none of this was her fault? I had so many questions with no answers, so I just clung to my Faith. Everything happens for a reason, and something good would come from our suffering.

The viewing was not as horrific as I had envisioned. No one turned their eyes, and no one made derogatory remarks about her appearance. She was the star angel of the show and was shown much love and affection. But when they lowered the coffin into the ground, I felt as if part of me was trapped in that coffin with her.

I do have a pleasant memory of that day, however. I have always felt the presence of those who have gone before us, and on the morning of the funeral, it just so happened that I needed to retrieve something from my grandparents' hutch, which was in my kitchen. I liked the hutch because it had lots of storage and was antique, and it held seldom-used items underneath and decorative ones on the shelves. But that day, I needed something from inside, and when I opened the door, the overwhelming scent of my grandparents' old home came billowing out. It was as if I were a child again, and there was my grandfather hugging me.

I immediately yelled to my mom, "If you need to talk to Grandpa Joe, he is living here in the hutch!"

It gave me a sense of peace that day, but I almost didn't make it through the funeral.

I wasn't supposed to be standing in a graveyard looking at the tiniest casket I had ever seen. I was supposed to be feeding, holding, and loving a newborn. My mind and my heart were at war because my heart wouldn't believe what my mind was telling me. Being in the cemetery, looking at the headstone of my husband's sister right next to where we were burying our three-day-old, and the finality of her not going home with us all came crashing down on my soul. When they began to lower Kaelynn into the ground, I felt as if I was going to implode into a million tiny particles, never to be reassembled the same way ever again.

I have never been the same. But, at the time, I didn't realize the strength I gained that day or the growth and blessings that were to come.

The very next day, my milk came in! Usually, this would be a glorious accomplishment for a new mother, as some women's milk never comes in. I should have been so grateful that my boobs were now hard and square, sitting like milky bricks on my chest. But they simply reminded me of the crushing truth that I had no baby to whom I could feed my mother's milk. I was in so much pain, physically and mentally. I nursed my wounds from being split open from hoo-ha to bunghole, nursed my hard, painful breasts while they dripped milk in the shower as the warm water washed over them, but I had no baby to nurse.

There was no baby for my empty arms, my empty womb, my broken heart. I watched several new moms being wheeled out of the hospital with balloons trailing and a lap full of baby swaddles, their husbands and grandparents following behind with bags, pillows, and presents. They all sported blissful Cheshire Cat grins. My lap was empty, my husband did not smile, and our dreams were shattered as we left the hospital with empty arms.

It is not lost on me how fortunate I am to have been able to carry a baby. There is no greater miracle than that of a healthy baby. I used to get very angry when I would see a pregnant woman smoking or hear that someone who wasn't taking care of the children that they already had was pregnant *again* with another healthy baby. But it is not my job to police other people's pregnancies or to judge how other people choose to live their lives.

I can only be thankful for the unconditional love and connection that I experienced with Kaelynn. It was like nothing I had ever felt before and like nothing I have ever felt since. I was her person. The only person that she knew inside and out.

I have always loved the quote by Dr. Seuss: "To the world, you may be one person, but to one person, you may be the world."

I was her whole world, and I will forever be grateful for that. There is no greater blessing than the opportunity to grow a person, except the opportunity and obligation that we have to share our story to give others hope. Little did we know at the time, but the end of Kaelynn's life was just the beginning of our beautiful story.

CHAPTER 4
MISCARRIAGE
(SOUR GRAPES)

We were never discouraged from trying to get pregnant again after we buried Kaelynn. In fact, we were encouraged after learning that Ellis-Van Creveld syndrome is a recessive genetic condition. It is an extremely rare recessive gene, with only 150 cases reported worldwide in 2007.[1]

Essentially, recessive genes are not always detrimental and can still produce beautiful results. The gene responsible for my blue eyes is recessive. My dad had brown eyes, and my mom has green eyes, but I ended up with blue eyes. This means that both of my parents carried a blue-eyed gene, but their more dominant gene resulted in their darker eye color.

There was only a 25 percent chance that Kaelynn's condition would happen again. In our grieving minds, there was no way that the horrible nightmare that we had just been through could happen again. God would not allow it. He would never be that cruel. I know

---

1. Paul A. van der Zwaag et al., "A Large Gene Panel for Heritable Thoracic Aortic Disorders and Related Conditions," *Orphanet Journal of Rare Diseases* 2, no. 27 (2007): 1–9, https://doi.org/10.1186/1750-1172-2-27.

now that it wasn't God being unfair or the devil trying to break my spirit; it was just what had to happen for God's grand plan to work—a plan so grand that I could never begin to imagine it.

But I digress, we (or I) decided that we should try to get pregnant right away. This was entirely out of grief, and I thought that the love of a new pregnancy and a new baby would relieve the pain of losing our baby girl. This is *not* how grief works, and not dealing with the pain of losing Kaelynn only magnified my sorrow. Concentrating on a second pregnancy distracted me from my original grief, but amplified the grief that was to follow.

When I say "try" to get pregnant, by the way, we never had to try very hard. I know that this was a blessing. I know countless women who had nothing but trouble getting pregnant, needed IVF, or had to grieve the dream of ever becoming pregnant. The agony I felt every time Kaelynn would move inside my womb, knowing she would pass away soon, is something that a woman who could never conceive would give anything to feel. Everything looks different with perspective. Everything feels different when the benefit of hindsight is applied.

I don't remember exactly how far along I was when the spotting started, but I remember immediately knowing that I was not pregnant anymore. I could feel it. I had failed again. At least that is what I thought at the time. Not only do I make sick babies, but I couldn't even carry this one at all, sick or not. What kind of woman was I? A real woman is supposed to be able to carry as many children as her husband can plant in her, and then she cleans the house, does the laundry, cooks the food, goes to work, and takes care of everyone without ever complaining or taking time for herself. Feeling less than had become a theme in my life. It started in childhood and carried through to very recently in my life.

Miscarriage often gets swept under the rug. If it is early enough in the pregnancy, you're only in love with a tiny fertilized egg—a little sack of fluid. But the moment you see that heartbeat on the screen, a flood of dreams, plans, and goals hits you before you have time to think about it. Especially if you have endured previous losses like I had. It made me wonder if the baby had the same condition that Kaelynn was born with.

Had God done us a favor by allowing us to miscarry? Was he trying to spare us from more heartache? Was he trying to tell us that we weren't meant to be parents? We weren't meant to have biological children? We could have just taken the miscarriage as a sign to adopt, or focus on our careers, or focus on each other. Maybe we should have healed from our first losses before we tried to get pregnant again. That was way too logical and would have made too much sense. That is not the route we took.

Let me be clear: I'm not trying to change anyone's mind about decisions they made in the past or affect decisions that they may make about the future. This is not my place. I just don't want guilt and regret to eat a hole in your soul. I felt guilty for so many years because I felt like it was my fault that my babies passed away. Stress has such a profound effect on our physical bodies. My body could not support a pregnancy when it was fighting to keep me alive. The mental state that I was in after we lost Kaelynn was the darkest fog you can imagine.

Imagine that you are constantly lost. You have lost your way, you have lost your connection to your spirit, and you have lost your ability to communicate effectively. The world around you feels like a dream state. Some days it feels like you are trudging through the deepest mud, and other days, everything feels harsh and cold, like the world is made of stones, and they are all tumbling down on top of you. Your world has caved in, your heart is shattered, your body is weary, and your mind is sick with grief, but everyone else just goes on about their business like nothing ever happened. If this is the way that I felt, how could I possibly expect my body to support another living being? I was a raw nerve. I was fighting to stay alive and didn't even realize it.

Just today, I realized why I am so obsessed with pictures. Pictures are my memories. Without them, I shut out all of my memories, good and bad. There are so many things that I don't want to remember. So many things that I never should have been forced to endure. If there is no picture, then it never happened. If there is no picture, then I don't have to feel it. If there is no picture, then there is no reason to be sad. Ask me how that has been working out for me.

I have become obsessed with documenting happy times. I used to be a complete basket case over family portraits. The outfits had to be perfect, the background had to be perfect, and the smiles had to be perfect—because we were happy, dammit, no matter how I felt on the inside.

Don't be like the old me. Be present, not perfect. Be free, not afraid. Be observant, not obsessed. These principles will allow you to experience joy again. They will enable you to digest your pain and detox it from your system. I have learned to trust my body instead of my thoughts or what others think about me. The only opinion I should care about is God's because even my own opinion of myself can get warped.

We all have trials, and we are meant to have troubles. Without them, we cannot discover our true strength or realize that the strength we found was not our own.

I'm so sorry if you have experienced loss, and while I may not know what that loss was or how it felt to you, I do know that there is a lesson that you can learn. I know it's an opportunity for you to find courage that you didn't know you had. Maybe it can be an opportunity to lean on God, because that is all He wanted you to do in the first place.

My lessons from my miscarriage were:

1. The plan is not mine.
2. You cannot rush miracles; they take time.
3. Rushing into the same situation that went wrong was not the solution.
4. There is always time to pray more.
5. Sometimes, not understanding is the only understanding I am supposed to have.

What lessons can you learn from your current or a past trial? Take some time to journal your thoughts right now.
The following **few pages have been** intentionally left blank; **please use them.**

_____

_____

_____

_____

_____

_____

_____

CRISTINA P SIMMONS

EAT YOUR FEELINGS

CHAPTER 5
KADYN, THE TASTE OF HOPE
(WARM VANILLA CUSTARD)

After we lost our first daughter and then had a miscarriage, we wasted no time getting pregnant. Or, I wasted no time. They still never discouraged us from getting pregnant again because, as I said before, there was a 25 percent chance of an unhealthy baby and a 75 percent chance that we would experience our dream pregnancy and leave the hospital with arms full of our bundle of joy.

To me, that meant: Let's go!

My husband was less enthusiastic. From this point forward, for a very long time, we were not on the same page. We were not even in the same book! But let's be very clear. His role in our marriage is to be the pessimist, and my role is to point him in the right direction, as I am the optimist. Most of the time, we balance each other. It is by the Grace of God that we've stayed together.

I became obsessed with having another baby after losing our first daughter. I am a people pleaser at my core, and I felt guilty. I felt broken. I felt like it was all my fault. This unyielding need to be pregnant would not go away. I can be a little obsessive, which will become more evident as our story unfolds.

I've always loved the notion of being pregnant. I have always known that I wanted to be a mother. My first pregnancy was my worst nightmare and likely more difficult than most everyone else's pregnancies. This was my warped perception: I was the only one who had ever lost a baby. I was the only one who would never have children of my own. Everybody else had happy, healthy, no-problem pregnancies. Right? I know now that is not reality, but then, I couldn't see any kind of reality through the fog of grief I was living in.

So many people are blessed to have uncomplicated, happy, healthy pregnancy experiences, but the majority of pregnancies have some sort of complications. They may be small complications or even a false test, but complications nonetheless.

Many people don't want to discuss complications in any aspect of life, but life is indeed complicated. Life is messy. Life makes you cry, but you learn to laugh again. There are a million uncertainties, but one thing is certain: In my mind, pregnancy is a miracle. It is truly a miracle straight from God.

We got pregnant very quickly again. My body had no trouble carrying a baby. I was very excited, and from the very beginning, I knew it was going to be a girl. Everything was going to be fine.

Everything was going to be fine.

The world could be on fire, but everything would be fine. Remember that I am the optimist in this story, the unrealistic dreamer.

I don't have many memories of Kadyn's pregnancy. I don't have many memories of anything. It's why I've struggled to write this book. I've talked about lack of memory before, but I just recently read that brain fog is a natural part of grief and can affect your memories.[1] This helped me realize this: Grief has stolen most of my memories.

---

1. "Brain Fog – A Physical Response To Grief," Buch Funeral Homes, April 21, 2023, https://www.buchfuneral.com/brain-fog-a-physical-response-to-grief.

But what I do remember is that I don't remember a lot about Kadyn's pregnancy. I remember a lot of the waiting, because there wasn't anything that we could do to see if the baby was healthy until I was around four months along. We had had an amniocentesis when we were pregnant with Kaelynn, and all it showed was a healthy baby girl. The genetic disorder didn't show up on the amniocentesis.

I do, for some reason, remember the shirt that I wore to the specialty hospital once the ultrasound was scheduled. I specifically picked it out. It was a pink striped maternity top, because I just knew it was going to be a girl. So, off we went to have the ultrasound.

In all of our ultrasounds, the technicians were very stoic. This is probably part of their training, staying impartial and not "diagnosing" anything during an ultrasound. I often pick up on people's energy, which can be very draining to me, depending on the energy. The energy in the room wasn't very good. We had the ultrasound. When they came into the room again, they said they believed this baby also had Ellis-Van Creveld Syndrome.

We had discussed prior, my husband and I, that in the event our baby was diagnosed with Ellis Van-Creveld Syndrome, we were going to abort.

I've been worried about including this in the book—it's a sensitive topic for many people. You have to understand I am a faith-filled person. I know that I'm not supposed to abort a baby, especially according to the Bible.

Exodus 20:13 says, *"You shall not murder."*

I chose to take the life of the very child that I had prayed so hard for. Who does that? I fully grasp that it is supposed to be God's decision.

As Jeremiah 1:5 says, *"I knew you before I formed you in your mother's womb."*

But if you have not carried a baby that kicked you every single day, sometimes every minute, and held her in your arms while she stopped breathing, I don't think you can counsel me on whether I should or should not have had an abortion. The mere thought of staying pregnant for five more months, knowing that this child, too, was going to pass away, was unbearable. I would have had no quality of life. I would have been unable to work. We probably would have gotten divorced, and, at the time, I didn't realize the state of depression that I was in.

I also know that our steps were ordered. God had a particular plan.

Proverbs 20:24 says, *"The Lord directs our steps, so why try to understand everything along the way?"*

I certainly did not understand any of this. None of this made sense. Why was it happening to me? And how could I just make it stop?

Someone, please wake me from this nightmare, I begged

These are times when we look to scripture.

Psalms 37:23 reads, *"The Lord directs the steps of the godly. He delights in every detail of their lives."*

Surely, He wasn't delighting in any of this, but this is what I do know: If we hadn't gotten pregnant when we did and we hadn't aborted when we did, we wouldn't have the children that we have now. They were supposed to be ours. We needed them just as much as they needed us.

This was the exact reason that we decided on the heart-wrenching reality of abortion ahead of time, because I knew that, in the moment, I wouldn't be able to make any decisions. I had already had to make some of the most painful decisions of my life at the age of twenty-five years old.

In the end, it was my body. I was the one carrying the baby. Nobody else could make that decision on my behalf. My husband had the luxury of detaching much sooner. If I am being honest, I never detached. That was part of the problem—why I had such a hard time processing the deaths. The father can detach. The father's body hasn't changed. The father doesn't experience the hormonal ups and downs that go along with pregnancy. He's not pregnant. So, we had already decided that, yes, we were going to abort.

The hospital could and would induce labor, and then I would have the baby "naturally." There was nothing "natural" about what was going on, but this was our reality. So we started the process of scheduling an abortion. Again, who does that? No one should have to do that.

And then the geneticist called. Apparently, our nightmare wasn't horrifying enough. The board had a meeting about my pregnancy and my body. They denied the request to abort. They would not perform the induction.

Unbeknownst to us, they had done some calculations, and at that time, they were uncertain about the rate of growth of the baby's rib cage. As previously mentioned, I was about four months at this point, and there was a cutoff as to when you could have an abortion. There were also other protocols in place, not previously discussed with us at the time, regarding whether it was detrimental to the mother's health. "Detrimental to the mother's health" can mean a lot of different things. So, in the hospital's terms, that is physical health. I found this information on the Mayo Clinic's website:[2]

"Your care team may suggest labor induction if you have:

- *Diabetes. This can be diabetes that came on during pregnancy, called gestational diabetes, or diabetes that was present before pregnancy. Having diabetes that's treated with medicine is a strong reason to consider delivery by 39 weeks.*
- *High blood pressure.*

---

2. Mayo Clinic Staff, "Inducing Labor: When to Wait, When to Induce," *Mayo Clinic*, March 12, 2024, https://www.mayoclinic.org/healthy-lifestyle/labor-and-delivery/in-depth/inducing-labor/art-20047557.

- *A medical condition such as kidney disease, heart disease, or obesity.*
- *An infection in the uterus.*
- *A body mass index of 30 or greater.*

Other reasons for labor induction include: Problems with the baby, such as poor growth. This is called fetal growth restriction."

There is no discussion of mental health. There must be guidelines and protocols, but no one invited me to the meeting about me. The board never discussed any of their findings or speculations with me. They just sent a messenger to deliver the verdict that had been made without me.

My mental health was already suffering. So, the option that they presented me with was going to an abortion clinic, which is not something that I was prepared to do, especially when I started to research the procedures that were available for this stage of pregnancy. The option that they presented to an already grieving young mother was to stick a very long needle, much like the one used during amniocentesis, through my abdomen, into my uterus, and into my baby's heart to kill her. I'm sure there was some kind of lethal cocktail in the needle, but I didn't feel the need to know any more about this option than I already did. Induction would still be needed because the deceased baby couldn't live in my womb after we murdered her with a large death needle.

This is what they decided to prescribe? I told them I wouldn't do that. The Lord heard our prayers, and the geneticist went before the board on our behalf and implored them to please perform the induction.

The real problem was that they didn't know. It was a very rare condition. I don't know what the numbers were in 2002 and 2003— when I carried Kaelynn and Kadyn, respectively— because I couldn't find any documentation on it, but I know that in 2007, there were only 150 cases reported worldwide.[3]

They didn't have much research on the syndrome. They didn't know how much her rib cage could or would grow. They also couldn't tell if there was brain damage at this point or if her organs would function properly. We didn't find out that Kaelynn had significant brain damage until after she was born. Kadyn's limbs were measuring as dwarfism at this point, so that was the driving factor for the diagnosis, but they couldn't tell about her ribcage or if it was going to be the same lethal condition as Kaelynn.

What was certain in my mind was that I had prayed, I had cried, I had talked with the love of my life, and the best decision for us at that time was the termination of the pregnancy.

It's strange the things I do remember. I remember the room that we were in. I remember that my husband had bought a motorcycle to piece together—like Legos, but a different brand. He wanted to have something to do while he was just sitting in the room, waiting for my body to respond to the drugs. I remember him working on it, and I can remember seeing him sitting in the lounge chair. They had a chair that almost folded out flat into a bed, so he could sleep in the room with me. I remember the room was very barren, not much on the walls, but there was a television, of course.

I don't even remember the pain of childbirth. I don't remember the waiting. I only remember when she was born, still inside the amniotic sac. I remember seeing that she was so tiny. I don't know how much she weighed, but it was ounces, not pounds. Her skin was translucent. You could see through it, but not quite. And her eyes were still sealed shut. She also had six fingers and six toes, like Kaelynn, and her arms and legs had a dwarfed appearance. She had

---

3. Jaafar, M., and Chouchene, M. "Ellis Van Creveld Syndrome: A Rare Case Report." *Ultrasound in Obstetrics & Gynecology* 62, no. S1 (2023): 365. https://doi.org/10.1002/uog.28241.

no hair anywhere on her body, and it felt like her skin was thicker than my own, even though you could see through it.

I do remember holding her, and that they dressed her in a little gown and preemie cap. There is a group of ladies who crochet little gowns and caps for preemies. I still have all of those from all three of our babies. I keep them in little boxes with their ultrasound pictures. They took newborn photos of her that we still have. I said I wanted to have pictures so that I could remember them; maybe this is where my obsession with pictures began. I didn't want to forget them because their lives mattered so profoundly to me. The images are no longer as difficult to look at as they were before.

But again, I failed. I failed again. That's what I thought. I failed to give my husband a daughter. I failed to give a grandbaby to my parents and my in-laws. Everybody was grieving again, and it just all felt like my fault. I knew in that moment that we were not going to have a funeral. She was so tiny that cremation was the only option. In hindsight, I wish I had cremated Kaelynn as well, so I could have her ashes with me, but that is water under the cemetery now.

I also remember being wheeled out of the hospital with nothing in my arms—again. There were other mothers and families leaving at the same time, but they were leaving with bags of presents, flowers, balloons, and a baby carrier. They seemed a little stressed and tired, but they were happy. Everybody was smiling and chatting about the events and what life would be like when they got home. We came in with despair and apprehension, and we walked out with empty arms and even emptier hearts, just like we had before.

You would think that, at this point, I would have just given up. I would have said we are not meant to have kids. This just isn't for us. I should have just tried to figure out what my purpose was going to be. I could have thrown myself into work or a million other things. I should have gone to counseling. That might have been a good idea. But I was still obsessed with having a baby.

This is the point at which I began to bring up the subject of adoption. We had talked through a dozen other scenarios. We could all undergo genetic testing to determine which parent on both sides carried the gene. We could have used donor sperm. We could have gotten donor eggs. All of those options still left us with maybe getting pregnant with a baby that was only half of one of us. That isn't what we wanted. We couldn't have what we wanted. Our plan was not the one that mattered. God knew the plan all along, and he had already set the miracles in motion.

My husband didn't want to hear about or talk about babies anymore. Nonetheless, I continued to be obsessed with trying to adopt somebody else's baby that they didn't want or couldn't care for. Did we want somebody else's baby that they didn't want?

I remember him saying to me, "I don't know if I can love someone else's child."

We would find out that wasn't true. But I understand the questions. Those are the questions I should have been asking myself. We probably should have discussed it more, but once again, it wasn't part of our plan. It was God's plan, but God hadn't let me in on the plan yet, so I was struggling.

Kadyn was born in May of 2003, and I don't remember much about the rest of that year except that I dreaded the holidays. I didn't feel like I had much to be thankful for, and Christmas wasn't going to be much fun to celebrate with empty arms.

I mentioned before that my husband's cousin and I were pregnant at the same time when I was pregnant with Kaelynn. Her son was born the month after Kaelynn passed away. That was hard. She knew it was hard, her family knew it was hard, everybody knew it was hard. He would be about a year and a half by the time Christmas rolled around, and everywhere I looked, everybody was pregnant. Everyone but me. That was my perception anyway: Everybody was pregnant or had just had a baby but me. Everybody else's dreams were coming true, and I was living a never-ending nightmare.

But God had a plan. We did have Kayden cremated and have her ashes in an urn shaped like an angel. For a long time, I had several urns on our mantle. I realized at some point that that probably wasn't the best place to have a bunch of dead babies and dogs. There they were, right in the middle of the living room mantle, displayed for everyone to see. But that was our life at the time, and I didn't want them to be forgotten. Their lives mattered, and mine was in jeopardy because I didn't know how to live without them.

That's why I was shocked when I found out that Kadyn would not be remembered with a birth certificate or a death certificate. When Kaelynn was born, we got both, so I assumed that the same thing would happen with our second child. Well, I soon found out that when your baby is born before twenty weeks, you don't get a birth certificate or a death certificate.

It was as if that baby never existed. But I had held her, I had her ashes, I had her picture, and I had her footprints. I needed a birth certificate and a death certificate. Kadyn's very short time on this earth was a very significant event in my life, and I was still searching for what her life meant to me.

It wasn't until the year 2017 that the Florida Legislature established a new certificate entitled "Certificate of Nonviable Birth." Families can now apply to receive this "birth certificate" in remembrance of their precious child.

2003 was the beginning of my spiral into anxiety and depression. Eating my feelings became my crutch, my coping mechanism, and the beginning of my mental and physical health decline.

CHAPTER 6
GRIEF, ANXIETY, AND DEPRESSION
(SALT AND VINEGAR CHIPS—THE WHOLE BAG)

Grief and anxiety started to consume my life at this time. I was furious. I couldn't believe that any of this was happening. It was so unfair, and we didn't deserve it. I didn't want to go to counseling. I didn't want to talk to anybody about it. I didn't want to talk to my family. I didn't want to talk to my friends. I didn't want to talk to my husband.

To be truthful, I didn't know *how* to talk to anyone about it, especially my husband. I couldn't talk about the losses without crying, and he didn't want me to cry. I didn't want to cry in front of him, so I stopped talking at all. This wasn't hard for me because I had never been very good at expressing my feelings. I was never invited to express my feelings when I was a child. I wasn't supposed to have any feelings of my own; I was just supposed to do and think what I was told.

My current attitude was that I knew what was wrong with me. My babies had died. That's why I was sad. Why did I need to talk about it?

Just to be clear, that was not the way through my pain. I obviously should have figured out how to digest my feelings instead of eating them, but I didn't have any coping tools or strategies, just raw, open nerve endings of pain and suffering. For every emotion, there was a food that would give me a false sense of temporary relief. My go-to emotion was anxiety. It was my most prevalent feeling or state of mind, probably due to my living in a state of fight or flight for most of my childhood.

Even in college, my dad was still a huge part of my life. I was still trying to make him happy, and I still didn't know who the heck I was, what made me happy, or what I wanted. I was always doing everything to make everybody else happy, so when we started losing children, those feelings were heightened. I couldn't do anything right, and I couldn't give other people what they needed. Taking the focus off me allowed me not to process all of the hurt.

Even though I had lost my way, I had not lost my appetite or my faith. I had not lost my hope, even though I was pretty angry at God for letting these terrible things happen. I was desperate, grasping at anything that would give me comfort, but refusing to go to counseling.

I don't recall praying specifically; it was probably more like yelling at God, telling him: *I prayed to You. I prayed to You about all these things that were happening. I prayed about what I should do. I prayed, and You said it was going to be* okay.

But I wasn't okay. I was so far from okay. I was so far from my husband and felt completely isolated. I felt utterly alone. This must have been the time when we were starting to talk about adoption, but I was angry, and my husband was tired of talking about anything that had to do with a baby. I was dreading Christmas because we were going to be with my husband's nephew.

I know this sounds selfish, but I didn't want to do Christmas. I didn't want to watch him open presents. I didn't want to watch him toddle around. I didn't want to watch her mother him. I didn't want to celebrate. I didn't want to celebrate anything. What was there to celebrate? I had nothing to celebrate. I felt like all I had were empty arms. All I had were broken promises. All I had was: *I'm not good enough. I can't make a healthy baby.* There were so many whys. Why was all of this happening? So I did a lot of things that I probably shouldn't have, to avoid my reality.

I ate. I kept putting on weight, and I justified it because I had just lost the baby. You know, you're supposed to be a little chunky after you have been pregnant, and my body was changing—all of those excuses that we tell ourselves. I was keeping things from my husband.

Grief makes you do bizarre things. I started going to a psychic. The Bible says that you're not supposed to seek out soothsayers, but I wasn't thinking about the Bible at this point. I just needed somebody to tell me that something good was going to come out of all of this.

So I started going to a psychic, and she had a gift. She knew things that she could not have known. The first time I went to her, she talked about my little girl walking hand in hand with an old woman who was wearing socks and flip-flops. There is no way that she could have known that my Abuela would wear my Abuelo's thick socks with her flip-flops. This is one of the only things that I remember about my grandmother. I also remember her beautiful, soft, white hair, which is where I think I got mine from. There is no way she could have known these details, but she saw my daughter walking with her, and so she had me.

She took thousands of dollars from me, and we ended up with a significant amount of credit card debt that my husband was unaware of. In my defense, I'm not sure he ever asked me how much the psychic cost. He probably didn't want to know.

But I was desperate, and I was hooked, and she kept feeding me more information. She kept telling me things she shouldn't have known, including things about my husband's sister.

One time, the psychic was repeating, "She keeps showing me a watch."

My mother-in-law once told me a story about how, after Christie passed away, they couldn't find her watch. They looked for it everywhere and couldn't find it. Then it suddenly appeared in one of the first places that she had looked, in her backpack. It was right on top, so you couldn't have missed it if you had looked in there before.

This psychic also predicted what would happen next, and I'll tell you about that later, but what I'm trying to say is that I should have been reading the Bible.

I should have been praying. I should have been writing down my thoughts and feelings and processing them instead of trying not to feel them, because I ended up losing thousands of dollars, keeping secrets from my husband, and the miracles were going to happen regardless. I should have trusted God, not a greedy psychic preying on my grief and insecurities.

So, there I was, thousands in debt and still anxious and depressed. Anxiety became a safe place for me. If I didn't feel anxious, there must be something coming to feel anxious about. This is how I was used to living.

This is how I lived as a child. I didn't necessarily want to go to school because I never felt like I fit in, but I also didn't want to come home, as I didn't know what kind of mood my father would be in. I didn't know if I was going to be in trouble for something that I didn't realize that I had done. I started eating my feelings when I was a kid. I felt comforted by food because I couldn't find that comfort in places or people.

I love my mom very dearly, and we have a very special relationship. However, I don't have memories of her from when I was little. I remember laughing, but I don't recall feeling like I could turn to anyone for comfort. Comfort wasn't a feeling that I ever felt from other people. I had to find other things to comfort me, and food was that something. As we say in the South, I got it honest, because my dad would eat to numb whatever pain he felt. I guess if he drank, he probably would have been an alcoholic.

Eating was a temporary high, like most addictions, I suppose. I would eat, and then that made me feel worse about myself. After we lost the children, I tried antidepressants for a little while, but because I was already chunky in the first place and they made me feel puffy, I stopped taking them pretty quickly. They didn't work for me.

I wasn't a never-leave-the-couch depressed person. I just went through life on autopilot. I tried to focus on anything and everything that didn't involve my current situation or what I had been through. I didn't want to talk about it. I hated small talk. Small talk was infuriating because it always led back to this: I buried three dead babies. And now I'm eating my feelings, and I'm pretty sure that my husband cheated on me. I was a joy to talk to. I didn't feel like I had anything in common with anybody—or at least I hoped I didn't.

Who would want to live my life? I didn't. I had friends along the way, but most of the friends that I've ever had, I haven't been able to keep because I couldn't relate to them. Everything made me anxious. I didn't want to be in the crowds and didn't want to go to parties. I didn't drink. I needed a real connection, but most people don't enjoy talking about dead babies. I didn't want friends who were escaping their problems. Yet, all I did was run, and everywhere I went, I was still there. Running from grief doesn't work.

Grief stole my ability to communicate, and anxiety stole my ability to feel close to people, to be intimate with my husband, and to let other people in. I'm not good at that. I hate hugging.

One of my girlfriends said, "You need to wear a sticker when you're comfortable being hugged."

I told her, "I'm not sure if I'll ever be comfortable with hugs, but to just keep hugging me anyway."

I know there is extensive research on the benefits of human touch and skin-to-skin contact, as well as the number of hugs we need to simply survive. I'm not arguing those facts, and I will admit that I do feel calmer after most hugs. I would much rather hug you than shake your hand because grief and anxiety have also made me a germaphobe.

I have started and stopped a lot of things because I'm constantly searching for that "something." Grief stole something from me that I can never get back, so I was constantly searching for something to make me feel better. Writing this book is helping me process some of that grief that remains.

Christmas is coming right now as I write this part of the book, and I'm feeling anxious. The best way to describe how I am feeling is anxiety, but I am also feeling some anger. You know what that means? I have been wanting to eat all of the crunchy, salty, sweet, and pudding-like goodies that are everywhere right now. I also just finished writing about the worst and best Christmas of my life, but that also helped to process some of those lingering feelings.

What I am trying to say is that sometimes you have to look within yourself, because that's where you'll find God—you'll find Him in your heart.

I was anxious, I was depressed, I was mad, and I was questioning everything, but I didn't want to do anything necessarily. So, I got stuck. There isn't any outside source that will make you feel better. There isn't any outside source that can take the pain away. You have to process it, you have to move through it. After I lost my children, I needed to feel safe again, because there had been very few times in my life when I felt truly safe. This is where I introduce the S.A.F.E. method, which is how I figured out how to do just that.

THE S.A.F.E. METHOD

Self-Care

Self-care has been my most significant game changer. I've had to focus more on myself and lead myself to be a better leader in my family, a better employee, a better wife, and a better mother. I've realized that I need to take care of myself first before I can take care of anyone else.

Self-care looks very different for everyone. You need to figure out what it looks like for you specifically. My version of self-care can change from day to day, and although it does include simple things like getting my nails done and massages once a month. It also includes non-negotiables, such as working out, walking outside, drinking plenty of water, and preparing my food weekly.

If I fail to plan, I plan to fail. I have come to know this about myself, so part of my self-care also includes telling others what I need. I never felt like I was allowed to have a voice, express my needs, or share my feelings when I was younger.

It's okay to have needs. It is okay to take time for yourself. It's okay to say "no" if you're too tired, too busy, or simply don't want to do what they're asking. Don't feel bad about yourself because you dislike what someone else likes. It would be a pretty dull world if we all wanted to do the same thing, the same way, every day.

Attitude

This may sound simple, but changing your attitude even slightly can make a huge difference. You've got to reframe your perspective. Do you have the correct attitude going into whatever situation you are facing or smack in the middle of? Can you shift your attitude? What can you learn from the situation by figuring out why you may have a poor attitude or outlook? Sometimes there is no "good" in a situation, but there is always God in every situation. Find His attitude or His perspective and apply it.

Feelings

You have to process them. You are going to feel the feeling whether you like it or not. It is going to suck, but if you don't deal with the emotions, they *will* deal with you at some point, usually at the worst possible time in the worst possible scenario.

I speak from experience because, along with approximately 11 percent of the population,[1] I used to have frequent and unexplained panic attacks. Pushing all those feelings into the abyss only allows them to fester until they eventually come to the surface.

You have got to figure out what you're feeling, why you're feeling it, how you can move through that feeling, and come out on the other side.

Energy

This encompasses all aspects of your life, including self-care, attitude, and feelings, which collectively influence the energy you emit into the world. If you put out yuck, that's what you'll get back. If you look for the doom and gloom, that is precisely what you will find.

I had to change my energy to attract people with the energy that I wanted to have. That may have been the most painful process because it has affected many of my friendships. I have loved all my friends throughout my lifetime, and some of them I've had for a very long time, and we've kept in touch, but it hasn't been a super-connected friendship. I know everybody gets busy, I understand that, but I was so wrapped up in my things that I didn't have room for anybody else.

This is also partly why I didn't want to take care of myself. I felt like that was being selfish. So, I had to learn how to lead myself and figure out what I wanted to be attuned to, in order to meet what others needed. Sometimes, this is still challenging for me, especially when certain situations trigger old wounds.

When you are a wounded momma, trying to raise yourself, it is tough to give your children what they need and raise them well. This

---

1. Cleveland Clinic, "Panic Attack & Panic Disorder," last modified July 13, 2021, https://my.clevelandclinic.org/health/diseases/4451-panic-attack-panic-disorder.

is still a challenging subject that I will address in more detail in the next chapter.

I am still in the process of giving myself what I need, which is a never-ending journey for all of us. However, I have learned that when I look at somebody else, I can see their pain, feel their despair, or know that they have a wall up trying to keep others out. I can feel a barrier, and I can relate to that. I can relate to why they feel that way, even if I don't know what happened to them.

It helps me to have more empathy for that person and give them more grace because I've been there, several times over. Now, at least I realize that my walls are retractable. I can raise one or put it down more on my terms. This is precisely the energy I was talking about. You've got to give off the energy that you want to receive, or you're going to end up with a lot of negative energy that you never wanted to be a part of. This can then cause you to have to process other people's energy along with your own. I don't know about you, but I have enough of my own to process.

CHAPTER 7
DANI AND DORI
(CHRISTMAS COOKIES)

Just before two of the greatest blessings entered our lives, I was overweight, overstressed, overmedicated, and pretty much *over it* altogether.

We had not even been married for five years and had already buried one child, had a miscarriage, and cremated a second child. These are not the dreams that marriages are made of, and it certainly took a toll on our relationship. My husband had pretty much given up on having kids altogether, and I was numb.

I was still working and existing, but life didn't seem real, and I lived in a fog. *Everyone*, it seemed, was either pregnant, had a baby, or was trying to have a baby. Everywhere I looked, there were pregnant bellies and smiling babies, and everyone was so much luckier and happier than I was. This becomes your truth when you are grieving. *Oh, woe is me, no one else has ever been through this, and everything is horrible and I hate everything, and here's my invitation for one to my big fat pity party!*

Underneath my blanket of gloom and doom, I still carried a little light for Jesus. I did my fair share of being angry with God. *Why me and why did this happen and why does everyone else have a baby and why, why, why, wah, wah, wah?*

This is the part where I blame all of this on my husband, because it is always a man's fault. Can I get an Amen? Just kidding, but I told him on more than one occasion that all of this is his fault. This was also the time when I started contemplating adoption. I blame my husband, but I should credit him with the miracle that happened, because if I had just never been able to conceive, I don't think he would have entertained adoption at all.

He probably would have done just about anything to "fix" me at this point. That is what many men do: they fix the problem. They don't stand around complaining and venting like we women do; they fix it. This couldn't be fixed; my heart was ripped open, my womb and spirit emptied, and I was withdrawing more every day. This marked the beginning of our slow separation, but sometimes the deepest wounds are made stronger by scar tissue that cannot be broken down.

I started the conversation about adoption, and he quickly shut it down with, "That can take a long time, and we won't be able to get a baby. Adoption is expensive, and I don't know if I can love someone else's child." I'm sure there were other arguments against the idea that I can't remember. In full Jesus-freak fashion, I knew in my heart that I needed to keep an open mind about adoption.

As a current student of spiritual awareness and seeker of all things that get me closer to Jesus, I am learning that the positive vibrations you send out into the world will come right back to you. I have believed for years that the energy that you put out into the world is the energy that you receive, and I have relentlessly, I mean lovingly, reminded my husband of this all the years of our marriage. Remember, my job is to be the optimist, and his is to be the pessimist, creating balance and conflict all at the same time.

Nonetheless, I told God, the universe, and anyone else who would listen that I wanted a baby. I knew that I was supposed to be a mother, and my unwillingness to give up resulted in the best Christmas presents any of us could have ever received.

This is one of my very favorite chapters in our life, and this book, because it is our girls' chapter. Our sweet girls, who may have just saved my life. Let me rewind to the conversation about adoption. I had started asking friends and family if they knew anyone who had adopted or had adoption connections. My husband's cousin had a friend who worked for a doctor in a town nearby who had been facilitating adoptions for years. The people in the doctor's office learned about our story, and I was encouraged to make an appointment to be added to their list of prospective parents.

It was getting very close to the holidays, and the nurse suggested that since the office would be closed through the holidays, I should call back after the first of the year, and they would set up an interview with the doctor. I thought that it would give us more time to consider our options, begin to make a savings plan and consider our living arrangements, which could use an upgrade.

I was settled with all these things, but I wasn't settled with the holidays. I should have been shopping for baby's first Christmas ornaments and cutie-patootie outfits, but instead, I was avoiding the "baby's room" and buying gifts for other people's babies, dreading spending the holidays with family and watching them open presents.

I wasn't sure that I could even "do" Christmas at all. I just wanted to stay at home and wallow in my misery, avoiding the sight of anyone else's happiness. If I remember correctly, I think I even asked not to open presents, and then at the last minute decided that I was being selfish and unfair. Christmas proceeded as planned, and I didn't have a breakdown, thank goodness. Sometimes the *win* is in just not having a breakdown.

I've left out a tiny, important bit in this story. My sweet husband loves me and is a very good gift-giver, but he has never been a real believer that he is. Every year, I make a wish list of sorts for him to choose from, and then he picks presents from the list and crudely wraps them in newspaper, scotch tape, duct tape, and any other annoying material that would cause me to spend hours opening them. He's always got the jokes. This particular year, I wrote "baby" about halfway down that list: Boyd's Bears, diamond necklace, CDs, baby, dance lessons, and so on. I thought maybe he wouldn't even notice. He shook his head and bought every other present on that list for me that year, and several of them were wrapped in duct tape.

That Christmas, we were at the grandparents' house all day, along with the rest of our family, including my husband's cousin. At 10 p.m. Christmas night, after we had returned home, I received a frantic call from my cousin-in-law. She had several messages on her answering machine (this was before everyone had cell phones) from the doctor's office informing her that twin girls had been born that morning—and they wanted to know if *we* wanted them.

This is the same doctor's office we had never set foot in, the doctor I had never spoken to, the doctor's office was closed over the holidays, but the same doctor who just happened to be on call Christmas day when a twenty-six-year-old cocaine addict walked in off the street in labor.

We embarked on a series of phone calls, starting with the doctor's office, which provided me with the attorney's contact information. I then called the attorney at approximately 11 p.m. She answered the phone, sounding enthusiastic and eager to help, and was willing to provide me with all the information I could handle at that time.

This is when I received the name and contact information of the social worker who would perform our home study—the home study that we were not prepared for, in the house that most would consider not fit for prematurely born twins with cocaine in their system. My mom was staying with us for Christmas and was there during all of this divinely designed chaos.

My favorite phone call is the one made to my mother-in-law. You can imagine the blubbering state I was in by this point, still shell-shocked and in disbelief at what was unfolding. A sob and a sniff followed my every word to her.

"There (sob-sniff) were (sob-sniff) twins (sob-sniff) born (sob-sniff) today (sob-sniff)and they (sob-sniff) asked if (sob-sniff) we (sob-sniff) want (sob-sniff) them (sob-sob-sniff-sniff)"

She, in her shocked and sleepy state, asked with all seriousness, "Can we just take one?" My immediate and certain answer was, "No!" They were certainly a package deal—identical twin baby girls born on Jesus' birthday. Not exactly what I had asked for on my Christmas list, but I don't look a gift horse in the mouth.

Have you ever heard the phrase, "Be careful what you pray for"? I didn't realize the true miracle of what was happening in that moment, but God had been planning this for some time. He knew these tiny girls would need a loving home, and He knew that we would send two girls up to Him. He took care of the twins in utero; their biological mom was incarcerated for the majority of her pregnancy. This meant that she was eating and most likely taking prenatal vitamins and, most importantly, not doing drugs for most of the pregnancy.

The girls did have cocaine in their system when they were born, which triggered the foster care system. Through another miracle, the doctor was able to convince the state that they need not step in because there was already an active adoption in place. The girls were tiny, one was four pounds twelve ounces, and the other, four pounds seven ounces. The runt of the litter, as we affectionately called her, looked like a little sack of bones.

Both girls had trouble with their suckling motion, and we needed to wait a couple of days for the attorney to obtain consent and release from the biological mother so we could officially visit. After that, we were able to visit, hold, and feed them almost every day. The nurses said this was important for them to know our smell and form a quick bond with us. I was immediately bonded of course, but my poor husband was afraid to hold them and always looked like the nurse was handing him a steaming pile of poop instead of a precious baby. He warmed up quickly and started to look increasingly comfortable every time he held one of them.

Way back in 2003, we weren't as concerned about germs. I do remember that we had to wear a backward hospital gown and wash our hands during every visit, but the gowns weren't even tied in the back. The girls weren't in the NICU or under any kind of special concern. There was some worry about them gaining weight, which is why they weren't released from the hospital for about two weeks after they were born.

But for all they had already gone through in their short lives, they were healthy. I'm sorry that I don't remember more about this time in our lives. I know that I was overwhelmed and still concerned that, even though a miracle was right in front of me, it might somehow be stripped away. I already loved them too much and not enough at the same time, in fear that they would be taken away from us. But, there wasn't time to truly process that because we had to get ready for them to come home.

Between visits, we frantically cleaned, straightened, and tried to make our tiny block home with drop ceilings and window air conditioning units more acceptable. I had heard horror stories about home studies and how strict the social workers were. Our social worker was lovely, and the majority of the interview focused on our beliefs about parenting and why we thought the other person would be a good parent. Isn't this really what matters?

My husband said the sweetest things about my heart and the love that I had to give a child. We will never see ourselves in the faces of our children who look to us for guidance, but we see love and trust in their eyes. We may not have created their physical forms, but we have nurtured their spirits and helped them become the sweet souls that they are.

Our home study went off without a hitch, and we were soon-to-be parents of identical twin girls. Was this really happening? It truly was a miracle, and I was living it, breathing it, getting nervous about it. We racked up the attorney's fees, passed our home study with flying colors, continued to make visits to the hospital, and on January 7th, two weeks after they were born, we got to bring our girls home.

I had a grand scheme. We left the Christmas tree up so that we could take pictures of the girls underneath the tree, like the best presents that they were. We were officially a family, and babies made four. It was blissful and perfect and everything that I had ever dreamed of, said no first-time parent of twins, ever.

I was happy and I felt blessed, but I was deeply exhausted. It had been a whirlwind since that phone call Christmas night. Mentally preparing, physically cleaning, and taking care of two babies as a first-time parent is no joke. Looking back now, the girls were probably experiencing withdrawal symptoms, and they hardly ever slept, which meant we hardly ever slept.

My mother-in-law took the night shift so I could get some sleep, but the cute little runt of the litter cried and cried and cried. The girls had some trouble with suckling, so from the day they were born, we had to work their jaws when they ate so they would pick up on the motion. This was extra work, and we had them on a very tight schedule so that one person could feed them if they were by themselves, which meant the girls didn't eat at the same time.

This was great in theory, but it would take one of them so long to eat that by the time you got the second one fed, burped, and changed, it was time for the first one to eat again. This meant that there wasn't much eating or drinking or "bathrooming" or sleeping for the big people in the house. It was twin care around the clock—all day.

I don't remember much about this time in our lives. We have plenty of pictures, and I remember the occasional funny story—like my mother-in-law pulling the bassinets from storage that belonged to my husband and his sister when they were babies so that we could use them for the girls. They were darling, and I was thrilled to be able to use them for the girls, but one night, when the girls were still tiny, their father put them down to sleep. I woke up early and always had to make sure that they were still breathing, because losing three infants and then adopting premature cocaine-addicted babies makes you a bit of a freak mom, just saying.

Well, the smaller of the twins was squirming around a little and whimpering. When I walked around the other side of the bassinette, I noticed that her arm was poking out between the rungs. As I picked her up, she began to cry, and that one arm was limp.

As you can well imagine, I immediately went to the worst-case scenario that my dark and broken heart could conjure. In about 3.6 seconds, I had (in my mind) called 911 while driving ninety miles an hour to the hospital to deliver my tiny baby with a broken arm to the emergency room, where they called child services, deemed me an unfit parent, and took the twins away forever.

This is where grief takes you, the fear that is in the darkest corner of your mind, that keeps you guarded and worried that the good thing that has been bestowed upon you will be ripped from your arms to leave you broken and sobbing again, and there won't be anything that you can do about it.

Meanwhile, back in reality, my husband woke up, saw the terror in my eyes and the limp baby arm, and somehow instantly knew that her arm was just asleep. She was crying due to the pins and needles of a sleeping limb that was beginning to wake up. Even with all the miracles that had touched our lives, I could still forget that God was in control and that I should trust Him. He had already seen our lives played out and had perfected the most glorious plan for us.

No, I do *not* know the secret to life that will be revealed when the Heavens are opened to us with angelic voices singing out, and all your worries will be lifted forever. However, I will provide you with practical tools and strategies to work through your pain in the chapters to come. I used to worry that I would be forever searching in this life for something that wasn't there to be found. So much had been taken from me that no matter what was given back, it wouldn't fill that hole.

Well, I am here to assure you that these feelings are wrong, that fear is a liar, and that the hole can be closed. It may not be filled with what was once there, but it can be knitted together with the gift of hope, the promise of Jesus, and the knowing that your faith will provide everything you need. I often wonder why I have been so blessed and how life seems to have worked out. But through it all, I have never forsaken my faith that God loves my family and wants only the best for us.

So, believe that miracles are real, that they can happen to you. One—two, really—certainly did occur in a tiny block house that Christmas. My girls filled a massive hole in my heart and continue to bless me by allowing me to be their mom.

I have some regrets, though. I got so caught up in caring for and loving my girls that I neglected to nurture and care for myself, my marriage, or my friendships. The pain and grief from the loss of my biological children were still there. The ever-widening canyon between me and my husband was still there. His unresolved grief from the loss of his sister was still there. The unforgiveness I had in my heart for my dad was still there. My countless insecurities and lack of emotional intelligence left me unable or unwilling to process adult problems or situations. I was essentially still a chubby twelve-year-old girl with no voice who always felt left out.

I was so focused on not letting anything hurt my girls that I sheltered them too much. I did everything in my power to keep them well, safe, and with me. Here is that "be careful what you pray for" scenario again: My girls feel so secure and protected in our home that they never want to leave it.

Fast forward to the present, 2024. In true helicopter mom fashion, I decided to find the girls their dream job. It turns out that it was only my dream, not theirs. In my defense, I had several photographer friends who assured me that the girls would make gorgeous models.

They would be, but they refuse to be models. I've tried everything. We spent thousands of dollars on acting classes, modeling classes, and a trip to Los Angeles. This came after many conversations and tears from me and the girls.

They were full of fear and anxiety about all the unknowns, flying on an airplane for the first time, and strangers judging them for their talent or lack of talent, and they were unsure of themselves. I was full of fear and anxiety about them never succeeding simply because they were too scared to try. I told them that I had lived most of my life in fear—first, in fear of failing, and most recently, in fear of succeeding.

I'm not sure that my girls will ever truly understand how much they are truly wanted. I cried, prayed, and pleaded with God to make me a mother. As soon as I released control to Him, my girls appeared out of thin air and saved my life. I have tried to live my life as an example to them—to show them that we can do hard things, we can overcome challenges, and we can help others in the process.

Currently, they are 21 years old, and they are probably going to be upset with me for putting this in the book, but I want nothing but light, love, and fulfillment for them. They haven't figured out their purpose yet, and that is okay. It took me a long time to figure out mine. So, I will support them in their interests and be the best role model I can until God whispers in their ears, just as He did in mine.

CHAPTER 8
DJ: DONNIE JR.
(SALTED CARAMEL CHEESECAKE)

Have you ever experienced an unyielding desire? I'm not talking about needing a piece of chocolate before you start your period or even wanting something crunchy when you are anxious. I mean a need that wakes you up in the middle of the night, a need that you can't stop needing, a need that creates a pit in your stomach, or a need that has completely consumed your every thought. In 2008, I needed to get pregnant again.

I should have been content, right? We had our beautiful Christmas twins, who were the light of our lives, and they had just turned four years old. Everything was great, or it should have been, but it wasn't. We were happy, right?

I have come to know that "happy" is fleeting; it is contentment that brings joy. We were as happy as we could be, I guess, because I still had not processed any of my grief from the babies we had lost, and I continued to pile on weight. I continued to be very anxious because now I had the girls, who I just knew were likely to die at any moment. You think bizarre things when you are grieving.

As a dysregulated, anxious, grieving mother of small children, I thought they would be taken from me like my other children had been. I smothered them and perfected the art of loving them too much but not getting too close all at the same time. I was very aware of who was or was not a part of their life. I was overprotective but not overly affectionate. I was never a mom who hugged and kissed my kids. I was so afraid I would get them sick, or they would get me sick. That's what I told everyone else, but it was really because I didn't want to love them "too much." Deep down, I was waiting for them to be taken away. My other babies were taken from me, and sometimes I thought that it was just too good to be true that I would get to keep our adopted children. I realize now that all of that sounds insane, but multiple losses and severe grief can warp your sense of reality.

I projected my anxiety onto them, which is one of my greatest regrets. It's not something that I can change, but I work diligently and tirelessly now not only to process my anxiety, but also to acknowledge theirs as well. I try to help us all work through it the best way we currently know how. It's a journey, and our anxieties won't go away overnight.

For the first four years of our girls' lives, we were a family. We had everything we had prayed for. We were able to move out of the very tiny house where we lived, where we learned how to be a young married couple, and where the girls lived as infants. The house had no central heat or air, a leaky roof, and solid concrete walls. It was fine for a little while, but we wanted more. I always want more.

We were finally able to build a house of our own, and it was located right down the street from where we had been living. We moved into the new house when the girls were about two, and it was stressful. Building a house is always stressful, but this was a time in our lives when we were living beyond our means. We had a lot of credit card debt, a lot to be anxious about, and I was still depressed. I tried to work full-time and raise the twins.

We had a nanny for several years. When the girls were still in baby carriers, and we were looking at daycares, I walked into one of the daycares with twins in tow, looked around, and thought, "I can't leave my babies here."

It wasn't because I was better than anybody else or that they deserved better than any of those babies who were there. I simply couldn't bring myself to leave them there. I didn't feel like that was what was supposed to happen. And so, a little angel in the form of a nanny appeared, and my girls got to stay home. They got to play in their pajamas, wake up late, and learned to walk and potty train all in our own home.

I'm very grateful for that, but I still felt like someone else was raising my children, and that wasn't something I wanted. I had always talked about homeschooling, which my husband disagreed with—he said that they wouldn't get the socialization they needed, and we just didn't know enough about homeschooling at the time.

We were so busy. Both of us worked full time, we had the twins, and we had just moved. There was just so much life happening that we forgot to *live* life together and to communicate with each other. So, somewhere in this chaos that we were living in, I decided that it would be a good idea to try to get pregnant again. Perhaps I was living under the delusion that it would bring my husband and me back together, but it also came from a deep-seated part of my soul.

I was driving in the car one day, and I suddenly felt a need to get pregnant again. I really couldn't explain it. My husband thought I was crazy (once again) and kept saying, "We're good. We have the girls. We don't need another baby."

I kept telling him that I just felt it. I felt like everything was going to be okay, and God was going to allow us to have our child. The girls needed us—that's why we adopted them, but we were meant to have our baby, a baby I just knew was going to be a boy. There were all these things that I just knew, even though I couldn't explain how I knew them.

I started working on Donnie when the girls were about two, and when they were about four, he finally agreed to try again. It was early

2008, and I was pregnant again. I had convinced myself that everything would be okay. I am the ultimate optimist.

When I was pregnant again, we had to go through all of the same motions: Waiting, waiting, waiting. We had to wait until I was four months along to get the fateful ultrasound. I don't remember details, but I am sure that I was blissfully avoidant of the notion that anything could go wrong—and oblivious to the fact that something was going to be wrong. And yes, something was very wrong, once again. The only thing I was right about was the baby being a boy.

I could not believe this was happening again. God had told me everything was going to be okay. It was all going to work out. It didn't work out, and we had to have another abortion. *That* was the hardest thing that I have ever gone through in my life.

Since Kaelynn, I have learned that some children with Ellis-Van Creveld Syndrome do live. It's a broad spectrum, much like autism and Down Syndrome, but they have a lot of heart problems, major organ problems, and physical challenges. I don't remember the hospital pushing back when we said we wanted to have the abortion. The baby's limbs and ribcage were very small.

The measurements of his ribcage were similar to those of our first baby girl, Kaelynn's. It was her ribcage that ultimately kept her from breathing. Even by some miracle, if this baby boy could live outside my womb, odds were that he would have ongoing significant health concerns. It wasn't just my husband's and my well-being that we had to consider now. We had twin four-year-old girls. If I had a child who was going to need around-the-clock care or multiple doctors' visits, it would not just change my life. I would have attended all the doctor's visits. I would have gotten him all of the available treatments. I would have done whatever I needed to do for him, but it was going to change not only my life, but the girls' lives.

God gave the girls to us, and I wanted to consider the ramifications that staying pregnant would have on them as well. I couldn't understand the reason or the good that could come from going through this again, but the good was not that far away.

My prayers had already been answered; I just didn't know it yet.

Donald Raymond Simmons, III, or DJ as we call him (Donnie Junior), was born on May 7th. We had him induced. I don't remember the date of Mother's Day that year, but I do know that it was shortly after he was born. When my husband and my girls presented me with a Mother's Day card, I ran off crying because I just couldn't deal with it.

I was so deeply in denial that this had happened a third time that I was ignoring the calls from the hospital to retrieve his remains. I didn't want to deal with it. I didn't want to have to cremate another baby. Then, on my husband's birthday, they called me and left me a different message. I didn't answer the phone again because I knew it was them. The message said that if I didn't call them back and give them directions as to what was to be done with his remains, they would dispose of him like he was garbage that just needed to be disposed of. You can imagine the state that I was in when I called my husband at work, on his birthday, completely sobbing, telling him that they were going to throw my baby in the garbage.

Somehow, I managed to call the funeral home and organize for them to go to Orlando to pick him up that day. I don't remember picking out his urn, but it is handsome and very masculine.

I wasn't in a good place, but I continued to slog through life in survival mode for the next month. Then, one day, my mom was at work. She thought it was like any other day, but that day would radically change the course of our lives and our family forever.

CHAPTER 9
JUDDSEN
(GLUTEN-FREE PIZZA)

I have come to expect miracles, but I am still astonished by the magnificence of God and the goodness that He has bestowed on our lives. However, at this point, I was tired. I was tired of being disappointed, tired of being sad, and tired of being tired. I'm not saying that I had lost my faith or my hope; I was just low on energy. My faith was soon to be renewed, again.

My mom asked me if we were going to look into adopting again after all the cremating and crying subsided. My answer to her was no, but if something fell into our laps, we would certainly consider it. So when one of my mom's fellow nurses asked, "How is your daughter doing? Are they considering adopting again?" My mom repeated what I had told her.

Her nurse friend then replied, "Here is one for your lap."

She told my mom that she had just visited home due to a death in the family. She was talking to her sister-in-law, who was currently working with a young girl who was six months pregnant. She was actively seeking someone to take her child because, not only was she six months pregnant, but she was also raising her eight-month-old daughter alone. Her mom was helping her with her daughter, but she did not have a partner, and neither of the fathers were in the picture.

You can imagine my mom's excitement, and she called me as soon as she could. Still in a bit of disbelief, I took the girl's name and number. I talked to my husband, who immediately said no. We had another set of friends who were trying and trying and trying to get pregnant and couldn't, so my husband wanted to give the baby to them. But I just kept thinking, *The baby wasn't presented to them. This baby was supposed to be ours.*

So, in true *me* fashion, I told my husband I had her name and number, and I was going to call her. My next words were, "If the baby is a boy, I'll have my answer."

His answer was still a hard, "No."

I was able to speak to her long enough to ask if she knew the sex of the baby. It was a boy, and I knew in the depths of my soul that he was meant to be ours. My husband was not settled with any of this and was not happy about the situation, but I pressed forward. This would be the beginning of the end of our communication. But my mom and I went to visit this pregnant young mother.

We sat across the table from her, and the first thing I saw when I looked at her was my husband's nose. Our skin tones were very much alike, and all three of us had blue eyes. I didn't realize it at the time, but she also had wavy hair. It was just the craziest thing—I felt like this baby was going to look like us. After he was born, he also had the bluest eyes, the palest skin, and very curly hair. Just like me. My girls have very olive skin, dark brown eyes, and dark hair. You can tell that they didn't come out of me, yet they were always meant to be mine.

Here's another wild detail: Our due dates were two weeks apart. I had DJ in May, although my actual due date was in September. I did not want to have another abortion, I did not want to cremate another baby, but if I had not listened to that unyielding voice that said I needed to get pregnant, we never would have found our son. We never would have found him, because we wouldn't have been looking. If we hadn't lost another child, we wouldn't have needed to look.

Against my husband's better judgment, we began the adoption process. He doesn't regret the decision now, but at the time, I think he was trying to keep us both from being hurt again. I tend to jump without looking into situations or when making decisions, but Donnie is very calculated and needs to fully process all options. We once drove to four cities and across three counties just to buy him a pair of tennis shoes. He doesn't make split decisions or rush into anything, so adopting a baby from a woman he had never met in person who lived in another state was definitely out of his comfort zone. But once again, he would do just about anything to make me happy.

We kept in touch with the mother long distance until the time neared for our boy's grand arrival. We packed up the twins, along with all our expectations, and found a house about thirty minutes away from the hospital. I was fortunate to be in the room during our baby's birth. Donnie was there as well, but standing around the corner so he didn't accidentally see anything that should have stayed private to the biological momma.

I cut Juddsen's umbilical cord and held him soon after he was born. These were all the dreams of a healthy birth experience that I had been longing for so many years. When I was going through the worst of times, I would often think, *What did I do to deserve this?* But now, in one of the most blessed moments of my life, I found myself feeling the exact same thing. Everything that had happened up to that point was meant to be. It had to be for that moment right then. It was never my plan, and I definitely was not in charge. I was certainly along for the ride, though, and trusted more than ever that God would always make a way.

Please know that we see this as one of the greatest blessings that we have ever received, but this was the beginning of our marriage slowly unraveling—the beginning of our disconnect with each other and our ability to communicate efficiently or at all. Adoption is beautiful, but adoption is expensive, stressful, and anxiety-provoking. There are so many unknowns. There are so many bills. Who knew we would be responsible for paying for the mother's maternity clothes, phone bill, apartment rent, medical bills, mental health counseling (if needed), all the attorney's fees—the list seemed never-ending. It puts a strain on any marriage, and it added to the strain we were already under.

I'm very well aware that you cannot put a price tag on the love you have for a child or the level of appreciation I have for Juddsen's biological mother. I have lost children, so I know the pain that she must have felt. It took great courage for her to admit that she needed help. I am forever grateful for her circumstances; her choices, good and bad; her trust in us, and that God led us to her. I pray for her often. But I also know that I was meant to be Juddsen's mom. God equipped me with the strength, the means, and the drive to better educate myself in order to understand what he needs. God covered me with His grace so that I could accept Juddsen's differences and his extraordinary abilities.

God put a dream in my heart to transform our struggles and failures when raising Juddsen into ideas and knowledge that would help other families like ours with their children.

You can't know what decisions you will make until you're faced with the most terrible of decisions. I truly believe in the deepest part of my heart that all of those things had to happen in order for us to find the son we have now. You will soon find out that he can be a royal pain in my butt, but I love him with all my heart. I would not trade him or our circumstances for the world; they have shaped who we are now.

CHAPTER 10
AUTISM
(GUMMY WORMS, NO ARTIFICIAL FLAVORS)

"You need to come pick him up or have someone pick him up immediately, and he will not be permitted to return to school."

This is the phone call that I received when Juddsen was in third grade. This was not the first incident or the first phone call I had received from this school or the many other daycares he had attended. I had developed PTSD-like symptoms when I heard a cell phone ring—the number of days that the school called me far outweighed the days when they didn't. The signs started well before third grade, however.

Juddsen was the best baby. Of course, when you start parenthood with premature twins who endured withdrawal symptoms from cocaine, one tiny baby born under relatively normal circumstances was a breeze. At least, we thought as much. There were early signs that we didn't think too much about. He didn't smile that much as a baby or imitate facial expressions. He was never one to snuggle or want to be snuggled by another person. He did, however, love to be swaddled very tightly. He hated footed or onesie pajamas and would scream, rolling around in terror until you took them off. He hated socks. He hated shoes, unless they were Scooby-Doo Crocs—which come in an infinite number of sizes, if anyone is wondering.

My husband and I had a screaming fight once over my mom buying him a larger size of Crocs. He screamed at me, and I quote: "Is he gonna wear Scooby-Doo Crocs to high school?"

I thought Juddsen would never make it to high school at that point. (I'm happy to say he is currently a sophomore in high school as I write this book.) He always played by himself. He loved to line things up in a row, but hated if anyone disrupted that line. He loved the feeling of being submerged in water, but couldn't stand the feeling of water rolling down his neck. He refused to wear a jacket and never complained of being cold. He would only wear a swimsuit on days when it would rain, because regular clothes were not meant to get wet. He would occasionally refuse to get out of the car if it was raining. He has always loved roller coasters and anything that mimics g-force.

He has only started to understand or exhibit genuine compassion toward humans in the past two years. He has always been more comfortable talking to animals than he has to other people. He can often live in an imaginary world and create logic from illogical circumstances.

Juddsen had severe separation anxiety from me from the time he was very young. His biological mom detached from him very early in the pregnancy because she knew that she needed to give him up. She always referred to him as "your baby" whenever we discussed the pregnancy. I don't blame her for detaching; it was the best way for her to cope with the situation she was faced with. I only bring this up because if children can feel detachment in the womb, imagine what they feel when they are outside the mother's body. As parents and human beings, we can have a profound impact on others with our energy alone. This will become more apparent and more important as we further explore Autism.

I was fortunate to bring Juddsen to work with me for his first couple of months, but eventually, we had to figure out a daycare situation. We were able to have a friend keep him for a little while, but then it became necessary to put him in a local daycare. He would scream as soon as I started to leave the facility, and I would cry all the way to work.

They would call me often, but not require me to pick him up. They would keep him in the office, but he still disrupted the entire school. Looking back, I always had good instincts as to why Juddsen would act the way he did. This helped me in the career that I have now. The classrooms in that first daycare were very small, and there was limited space for the kids to move around.

Remember when I said that Juddsen hated footed pajamas? When he felt confined, he would try to escape, and if he was not allowed to escape, he would scream, and scream, and scream. Sometimes I can still hear him screaming, even when he isn't screaming. He screamed a lot when he was younger—in the grocery store, in restaurants, in church. We would do almost anything to get the screaming to stop.

We avoided most outings for a long time, but God became an integral part of our routine. We needed to be in church, but our anxiety levels were high. All I could think about was when they were going to call me out of service because Juddsen was screaming, and they couldn't get it to stop. Our journey back to church and community outings was a long one. I could probably write an entire book on the benefits of Walt Disney World for families with children who have challenges. We learned a lot from family trips to Disney and found great joy, though our experiences may have been different from those of typical families.

God has always encouraged me along the way. Children's church has these little tags that they put on the kids' backs so they know which parent belongs to that kid. The numbers and letters on them are random and picked by a computer. The sermon that particular Sunday was titled "Get Past Your Past." That Sunday was also my husband's birthday. I looked at Juddsen's tag and saw "DJ7" on it. Donald Raymond Simmons, III, was born on May 7. Donnie and I are the only ones who call him DJ, for Donnie Jr., I immediately knew that this was a hello from Heaven. That gave me a lot of peace that day.

But I'm getting ahead of myself. We knew that Juddsen was different from about the time he was two-and-a-half years old. We would find him lying on the floor, staring at the spinning wheels, watching them turn around and around. He liked to play by himself and did not enjoy being around other kids, which was one of the reasons he had so much trouble in daycare. He didn't understand how the other kids thought, especially when he was at daycare with kids of all different ages. He wasn't tolerant of children smaller than him. He didn't understand why the "babies" didn't slide down the slide faster. One time, he threw one off the merry-go-round because she was in his spot.

He was just different from the other kids, and, for a long time, that hurt my feelings. I didn't like the fact that he was different. I especially didn't like the fact that I got calls from the daycare every day. But the reason that we decided to get him diagnosed finally was all the trouble in pre-K. I was getting repeated calls from the teacher, who was incredible. She was trying to understand him, and she was trying to work with us, but we didn't even understand him or know what he needed.

On one particular day, something upset him. They were coloring, and he wasn't allowed to choose the color that he wanted. His favorite color is green, and to him, there is no other color. Maybe one of the other kids got green and they handed him a different crayon. Whatever the exact scenario, it didn't go well, and he flipped over his chair, kicked the trash can, and scared several of the other kids with all of the screaming.

This wasn't the first incident, but at that point, the school called a conference. They knew that he wasn't a bad kid, and there was something else going on. For teachers and therapists in the school system, it isn't always appropriate or accepted to ask if a child has been diagnosed. But sometimes, leading a parent to where you want them to go can be helpful for all parties involved. I would have welcomed someone being very forthcoming with me back then because I was lost. I had no idea why he was acting the way he was. I had never seen a child act that way. My girls certainly didn't act that way. They were just the sweetest little angels you'd ever met, at least most of the time.

I don't remember the entire process of how we picked the specialty hospital. The pediatrician gave me a referral list; we did some research and a little praying, and we landed on one that was relatively close. It was still a good hour and twenty minutes from where we lived at the time, but their testing was comprehensive. We spent the entire day undergoing all the tests, visiting all the doctors, and consulting with therapists. Then they all wrote up their reports, and several weeks later, we went back to get the results.

This whole process was very traumatic for me, and thinking back on it now, I tried to act brave. After all, we'd been told three times that our baby was going to die, and we were comfortable with something being wrong with our child. At least, that was what I told myself. But I wasn't okay with it. The day we were going to get the results, I went to the gym that morning. I was so stressed out that halfway through my workout, I just started to cry, and I couldn't stop.

I needed to cry, which I tried not to do very often because I thought that was a sign of weakness. I just cried a couple of minutes ago while writing an earlier chapter. It's cleansing (so cry if you need to).

Before we left for our appointment, I fought with my husband because he didn't seem like he was in a hurry to get there, and it was a very long way away. I hated to be in the car. I hated traffic. I hated the turnpike. I hated the interstate, and all of those things were happening in one day.

We finally arrived and got the official autism diagnosis. In 2012, four types of autism were recognized: ASD, or Autism Spectrum Disorder, Asperger's Syndrome, childhood disintegrative disorder, and pervasive developmental disorder-not otherwise specified (PDD-NOS).[1] Juddsen was diagnosed with Asperger's Syndrome. I found several books written about Asperger's or by other people who had been diagnosed with Asperger's. Juddsen had all the classifications and characteristics of Asperger's Syndrome, but in 2013, all four diagnoses were consolidated into one category: ASD.

No matter the classification or category, the diagnosis still allowed us to get him services. I spent the next twelve years researching and educating myself on how to help him navigate the world as he sees it. Because even after we got his diagnosis, it didn't make things much easier.

We made it through pre-K and got to kindergarten, and we had a fabulous teacher. I'm very grateful to all the teachers at that school at that time of our lives because they tried their very best, and they did love Juddsen, just as they had loved my girls.

But there wasn't as much education for teachers and school leaders in the school system on neurodivergent kids, and there weren't many advocates either. Juddsen was attending a charter school when he was diagnosed, and they weren't equipped to assist him with extra support systems at the time. I had checked into the E.S.E. (Exceptional Student Education) programs at some surrounding schools, as well as a local school for autistic children.

But at that time, he didn't fit any of those molds. Juddsen was very smart, but very socially awkward, easily triggered, and very

---

1. Autism Speaks, "DSM-5 and Autism: Frequently Asked Questions," accessed May 13, 2025, https://www.autismspeaks.org/dsm-5-and-autism-frequently-asked-questions.

sensory-driven. Every day, there was some kind of meltdown because he transitioned poorly, not only in school but at home and in most community situations. Whenever he would begin a task, whether it was play or school-related, he needed to finish it. His perception of finishing didn't always align with mine or his teacher's, which often caused problems and led to meltdowns.

The charter school was very fast paced. The kids were expected to move at a pace that didn't allow for extended transition times. Juddsen needed extra cues and extra time. He just needed more support than the other kids, and he needed more support than the one teacher in the classroom could give him at that time. We made it to third grade at that school.

By the time Juddsen entered second grade, I had accumulated a lot of data about autism, received countless phone calls from the school, and had plenty of sleepless nights. I wanted to contact his second-grade teacher first thing so that she knew what she was getting into. I also wanted to ensure that we were familiar with each other and would communicate from the start.

She was so sweet. The night we went to the "meet the teacher" event, I asked if she had seen Juddsen's file. She probably thought I was a typical helicopter mom, and that I was overreacting. She said that she usually gave the kids a couple of weeks to adjust. Then, if we needed to have a parent-teacher conference, she would schedule one at that time. I think we made it three days before she contacted me for a conference.

Anytime there was a weekend, a holiday, summer break, or a change in the schedule, it was as if Juddsen had never been to school before. I didn't decide to go back to school to become an occupational therapist until he was seven. By this time, I had PTSD from my cell phone ringing. I was actually in my class when we got the call that I started this chapter with.

It was consuming my life. It was consuming every corner and every crevice of our lives. I fought with my husband all the time because he didn't understand how Juddsen processed information. He thought that Juddsen was being defiant, not listening, or just being a brat. I kept trying to explain to my loving husband, especially the more I learned in school about occupational therapy and neurodivergence, that our boy just did not think the same way that we did. It often turned into a power struggle, so I was picking my battles with my son and my husband.

I was trying to give Juddsen the space and the time he needed to process things, but to my husband, it looked like I was being too easy on him, or I wasn't giving him consequences, and he was running the household. I certainly was not perfect at "treating" Juddsen back then, and we still struggle with him in certain areas to this day. However, I quickly realized that yelling at him or giving him ultimatums was not effective.

That's not how his brain processes things. He needs to have choices. He needs to know when the schedule is going to change. He couldn't handle multiple commands or instructions at once.

These needs, coupled with behaviors I observed in the clinic setting, were the inspiration for the C.A.L.M. Framework. It has truly changed the way we navigate Juddsen's needs as well as how I navigate my own.

C.A.L.M. FRAMEWORK

Chunk

"Chunking" tasks simply means breaking them into smaller parts. Juddsen often had episodes where he would shut down when presented with multi-step tasks or an entire page of math problems, for example. He refuses to do any part of the task or any of the problems because he assumes it will take him, and I quote, "forever." To make it more manageable, we give him one or two directions at a time or cover most of the page so it doesn't seem so overwhelming.

Adapt

This can mean adapting the environment to be more calming or more (positively) stimulating—whatever the case may be. It can mean adjusting where you are sitting or the chair you are using. For kids, this can even mean moving to the floor. You may need to adapt the length of the activity or shorten the list of to-dos. Change the activity in any way that will cause less anxiety or a feeling of overwhelm.

List

Making a literal list can be very calming. Everyone knows precisely what is expected and what will come next. It also brings a great sense of accomplishment when you can check off each task as it is completed. This seems extremely simple, but the majority of the time, that is exactly what our son needs—simplicity and security in repetition or structure.

Movement

We all need to move. Moving grounds me and calms my nervous system. My son loves deep pressure, but pushing and pulling a heavy weight can give the same effect. The neurodivergent brain does not enjoy being still. Action can equal organization in a sometimes disorganized system.

Proprioception (the sense that tells us where our body parts are in space) can be difficult when the nervous system is dysregulated. Movement and resistance help regulate the nervous system so that we can focus on the task at hand.

Using the C.A.L.M. Framework, even loosely, has been a real game changer in our household. And as much as I love the comical aspect of my son's literal interpretation of almost everything, it can make life challenging sometimes, even in the simplest situations.

This is probably a good place for a funny story. We were once driving to Target, and Juddsen was in the backseat, certainly on some kind of gadget—a Nintendo DS, tablet, or iPad. I used to get terrible looks in the grocery store because I was the mother who allowed my child to be on a tablet. But it was necessary to keep him from screaming while I shopped; the groceries won't buy themselves, so you do what you have to do to make it through the day.

When we pulled into the Target parking lot, I said something simple like, "We're here." Juddsen didn't respond because he was looking at his gadget.

I then very cheerfully said, "Hey, are you ready, Freddy?"

He looked at me with sheer terror in his eyes and asked me if I had forgotten his name. Then he began to ramble about how he didn't understand how that could be possible. I had never called him that before, and why would I call him that name? It wasn't even close to his actual name. He was almost in tears. I had to stop him and tell him I was so sorry. I explained that it's just an expression and that I didn't mean anything by it. I told him that, of course, I knew who he was. He was my son, he was Juddsen; I had given him that name, and I loved it.

Sometimes, I have to be careful what I say because he will take it to heart. We are a pretty sarcastic family, so through the years, as he has matured, he has learned to pick up on some of the sarcasm. His sarcasm is still different from ours, but there is hope. But we still have to be very careful when giving him directions and cautious about joking around. If there is something important that we need him to do, we use the C.A.L.M Framework.

We also go over plans the night before so he knows what's going to happen the next day. Our lives aren't always thoroughly planned out, but we like to have a loosely laid-out plan, at least. Our lives have been joyful, but we have to prepare a little more than most families. We also have to renegotiate and over-practice scenarios to avoid meltdowns.

After Juddsen was dismissed from the charter school in third grade, we had no idea what to do next. The school didn't give us any real direction. After a bit of research, I found out that, yes, we did have to have him in some kind of school for the rest of that school year.

Thankfully, my mother-in-law was able to homeschool him online for the remainder of his third-grade year. My girls finished out their school year, and then we disenrolled them from that school as well. For his fourth-grade year, we decided to send all three kids to a private school. I was able to get a scholarship for him with his diagnosis. This paid for Juddsen's portion of the private school tuition.

Our girls never loved school, either. Dani, in particular, consistently struggled in school. I even took her for testing under the suspicion that she was dyslexic. She had short-term memory loss and recall delays. She also had trouble formulating thoughts in her brain, and then either speaking them or writing them. She still has difficulty making decisions, both big and small.

We realized that a private school would be a much better place for both girls, so God worked it all out. We did the private school route for a year. It was still a struggle. Juddsen was in a portable classroom, which was a very confined space. There was barely enough room to move between the desks. It brought me back to that first daycare situation where he felt very confined and wanted to escape all the time. He wasn't doing much of the academic work in that classroom, and the teachers were just trying to keep him from having meltdowns, so they didn't push him.

After a year of private school, we then made the difficult decision to put him into an autism school. Juddsen was never very good at making friends when he was in the other schools. He didn't relate to the other kids, and the other kids didn't understand how he thought. He started to notice that his sisters had friends, and he began to question why he never had sleepovers or why only family attended his birthday parties. One day, he came home talking about Charles this and Charles that, and Charles said and Charles did, and me and Charles, and Charles is so funny! So I finally had to ask who Charles was.

He looked at me very matter-of-factly and said, "You know, my best friend Charles!" I almost cried because he had never really had a friend, let alone a best friend. Charles was the absolute best thing that came out of that autism school.

When he was a freshman in high school, I started to work at his school as an occupational therapist. I was able to take a closer look at the academics offered there, and while the curriculum was challenging for the majority of the kids, it was no longer challenging for our son.

Those of us in the personal development and entrepreneurship space often say, "If you're the smartest person in the room, it's time to find a new room."

Juddsen had become one of the most intelligent people in the room. So, much to my dismay, and with a severe spike in my anxiety levels, I heard that little voice in the back of my head. It said, "You need to put him in the public high school."

I am very proud to say that Juddsen now attends public high school. Join me in congratulating him for being invited into the National Honor Society and contemplating taking honors classes. He is not certain he wants to take on that much responsibility (ha, ha). I never thought he would be able to navigate high school on his own. He now has a cell phone. He keeps up with his classes—as much as a typical teenager does. He has learned precisely what he needs to do to get by with a "B." So that is what he does. He figured that out all by himself, and I am so very proud of him. I can't wait to see what he does in this world.

I am currently contemplating starting a nonprofit for churches across the country. We have created a "sensory room" at our local church for kids who need extra support in the church environment. I had a vision that we would name it "Juddsen's Room" and that there would be sensory rooms like this one in churches all across the country, which we would help to fund and raise money for.

We were unable to attend church when Juddsen was little. That means that we also missed out on having the girls in church when they were young. When we did try to attend, I would be called out of service every time because Juddsen was screaming or having a meltdown. That's another reason for writing this book. It's another reason why I want to speak about this and tell our story. I want to help those parents who hear their child screaming even when they are not. I want to give them hope and let them know that Juddsen now sits next to me in the pew during church.

I thank Juddsen for the lessons and the drive he gave me to keep educating myself. I'm grateful that I was able to accept what I couldn't change about him to transform his challenges into the beautiful person that he is today.

CHAPTER 11
CANCER
(STALE SALTINE CRACKERS)

My road to physical and mental wellness has been a *long* one. I am no stranger to pain. In fact, pain has been a faithful companion to me for most of my life. There have been more times than I would care to count that I have had to accept that there would be pain.

I'm much better at enduring physical pain than mental anguish. I endured a series of excruciating surgeries in 2015 and thought I had moved past the chronic pain. But a recent physical healing protocol brought back some pain I didn't even realize was still with me. Let me start from the beginning, again.

I had just been accepted into an occupational therapy school to be an assistant. I had decided that I wanted to go back to school for occupational therapy because we needed help with Juddsen. I had called several places after his diagnosis, and there was a waiting list at every one. There were no occupational therapy services anywhere near us, and no one would come to the house. I just kept hitting dead end after dead end. Some clinics wouldn't even answer the phone, and I couldn't leave a message.

Looking back now, it was probably God closing all those doors so that I would be funneled onto the path I found, which was going back to school to better raise our son. And this is what I did.

The program was in-person, but since it was for an associate's degree, it was technically part-time. You know the saying: "There is no good time to have a baby"? Well, there is no good time to go back to school either. You just have to do it. So, if you are feeling the tug to go back to school and that is what you truly believe God wants you to do, figure it out. That is my PSA for today. He will make it happen if He promised it to you.

I already had a bachelor's degree in biology (the bachelor's degree that my mom thought would be useless). When I changed from my first major to biology when I went to college in my twenties, she so lovingly asked me, "What are you going to do with a Biology degree besides wipe your ass with it?" So, thanks, Mom, for that, because it did give me a little fuel to do way more with it.

That "useless" degree got me into the OTA (Occupational Therapy Assistant) program without having to take any prerequisites. God knew that I already had everything I needed to start.

I could just go straight into the program, but this meant driving five days a week to downtown Orlando, where the traffic was terrible. At this time in my life, I had a severe phobia of being in the car and on the interstate. So why not combine two of my biggest fears and repeatedly confront them, five days a week, for weeks on end?

God was working everything out, though. My job at the time allowed me to attend school from 8 a.m. to 12 p.m., then head to my job at 1 p.m. and work until 5 p.m. Now, I know you're doing a little math in your head. That means I was either in school or at work all day. Did I mention that I needed to leave the house around 6:30 a.m., or I would get stuck in traffic and be late for class?

I still had three kids. I still had to eat. I still had to study and complete school projects. I was scheduled to start the program in August 2015. Donnie was supportive and ready to be Mr. Mom for a little while, and I was prepared to do the hard things to accomplish my goal. After all, we had been through much worse than this, right? We had weathered the storm of infant loss, depression, autism, and panic attacks. God certainly wouldn't test us with any more obstacles, and I would sail through school with no problem. Well, that certainly was wishful thinking.

My birthday is July 15, and I had gone to the orthopedic doctor to get a shot in my left knee that was bothering me. From the time that I was old enough to run, Dad had me and my sisters in some kind of sport. All three of us played soccer. I played basketball for a little while, but I wasn't very good at it. We played softball locally and on travel teams. I ran track in high school. We were always on the move for one sport or another. I didn't always enjoy the sports, as you'll recall from Chapter 1, but I did love indoor soccer, or simply "indoor" as we called it.

One day, while playing indoor in high school, somebody pushed me into the bleachers. I landed on my left knee and cracked my collarbone. That was painful. Mine was only a hairline fracture, but it doesn't matter which way you move; you are going to feel it in your cracked collarbone. Everything is connected, literally, in your physical body as well as your mind and spirit. So, long story short, I had to have surgery on my left knee, which was worse off than my collarbone. I had a cracked patella, torn meniscus, and deterioration underneath my kneecap—and my patella was off center. This was something I was born with, but the doctor decided to fix it since he was already slicing up the rest of my knee. I had trouble with that knee from then on, eventually having a second surgery to remove the scar tissue from the first surgery.

Those surgeries were both in high school, and I recovered pretty quickly, but I would have several shots of cortisone and fluid drawn off that knee over the next fifteen years. As I was preparing to start the occupational therapy program, the issue was bothering me again, and I knew that during my training, I would have to transfer patients as part of the testing and clinical fieldwork.

I went to get a cortisone shot like I had done several times before. Easy peasy, in and out, right? The doctor, whom I will forever be grateful to, took X-rays that day. I'll have to send him an autographed copy of this book, because without him, I may not have been here to write it. He showed me the X-ray of my left knee, but there was a tiny part of my left femur showing as well. He told me that I had arthritis in there, but then he pointed to the bottom part of my femur, and said, "See these white spots? Those aren't supposed to be there."

My next question was, "Well, what is it?"

He told me that he wasn't sure, but I'm fairly certain that he knew and just didn't want to mention it to me at the time. He didn't want to scare me. Instead, he referred me to a specialist in Orlando. Not long after my appointment with the first orthopedist, the school called for my final preparations to start in August. I had no idea what was going to happen with my leg. My intuition was telling me that I would have to have surgery, and so I postponed starting school.

I was discouraged because I had been so sure that this was the path God told me to take. This is what He told me He wanted for me and my family. I didn't understand why it was being blocked.

I went to the specialist in Orlando. They did more X-rays. They did MRIs. And then they did more MRIs. The doctors and technicians were acting very strangely and being very secretive. They kept asking me the same questions repeatedly. Some of them even pushed on my thigh and asked if it hurt.

"Can you feel this? Does it feel different than it did before? When did this pain start? Was there a time that you didn't notice it?"

I don't suppose that the questions themselves were strange, but the way that the doctors approached me was strange. I knew that look. That look that people give you when they are about to announce a death sentence. I remembered that look from when we were pregnant with Kaelynn. But, as usual, I was the optimist and just pretended that everything would be fine. It's all fine. I'm fine. You're fine. Everything's fine. The world's on fire, but it's all fine.

This particular orthopedic specialist had received terrible reviews because his bedside manner left much to be desired. However, in his line of work, you need to get to the root of the problem. This philosophy can be adopted in all aspects of life. Get to the root of the problem, make a plan, and move forward because sitting in "poor pitiful me" mode doesn't get you to a solution.

No need to sugarcoat things for the Simmons. We were good at hearing the hard things. We had doctors tell us three times that our infant was going to die. We were good at identifying the problem, outlining our options, and devising a plan that would move us through it. We knew how to do that. So, when he told us that I had a tumor growing from the inside of my left femur bone, that I needed to get on crutches immediately, and stop putting any weight on that leg, we did just that. The tumor was bowing the bone from the inside out, and the doctor was afraid that my bone would break, and whatever was inside could spread to the rest of my body.

Remember in Chapter 2 when I told you Donnie was beginning to take our health more seriously and dipping our toe into the self-development world? That started me on a path of tough workouts. I had been deadlifting 200 pounds and easily pushed my body weight and more on the leg press. I was doing box jumps, pistol squats, and running nearly every day. All of that had to stop when I was told to keep all weight off my leg, but, in the moment, I was okay with that because I was in "let's make a plan" mode. Let's push past this and get on with life.

But if I am being candid, I was in denial. There were many things going through my mind. The doctor did give us some technical jargon and information on chondrosarcoma, the bone cancer I had. He proceeded to inform us, in his straightforward bedside manner (he had no trouble scaring me), that the majority of chondrosarcoma cases end in amputation of the limb in question.

So, I asked him, out loud, "What other options do you got, Doc? Because that's not happening."

He replied that before options are discussed, we first needed to schedule a bone biopsy. So now I was not only facing one surgery, but at least two, and possibly amputation of my left leg. The bone biopsy was necessary to take a sample of the material that was inside my bone to figure out precisely what it was or was not. After conducting some research and self-education, I discovered the reason why all the other doctors at the imaging clinic kept pressing. Bone cancer is usually excruciating. I had had surgery on that same leg twice in high school, so that leg and knee always hurt. Although I wasn't having any more physical pain than I usually did, the mental pain started to wear on me.

During all of this, I forgot that it was my job in our marriage to be the optimist. I got pretty angry, but I wasn't telling anyone that. I tend to keep my feelings to myself, which is why I often stuffed them down with food. I told God how angry I was, but with everyone else, I was just quiet, or I cried. I couldn't understand why this was happening. Hadn't I already endured enough pain? I had buried or cremated all three of our biological children. I loved the kids that we had now, and I knew that they were supposed to be ours, but raising them was beyond difficult. Our marriage had already suffered greatly, and we finally seemed to be getting back on the right track. It was just all too much for me to process.

The shower is where I get a lot of my downloads. I think it has something to do with the water—there's also nobody else in there, it's quiet, and I don't have to think about the fourteen thousand million other things that need to be done. This is when I hear from God the most easily. This particular day, I was yelling at Him (inside my head, obviously) while standing in the shower with the water running over me, sobbing. Asking him why.

What could I possibly learn from this? Why do I have to go through so much more pain? There were still some unknowns at this point, but one thing I was certain of was that it would hurt. There were so many thoughts swirling around in my head as I stood there crying and watching the water go down the drain, much like my hopes and dreams.

Then, all of a sudden, I was snapped back to reality when a very clear message popped into my head: "*This* is what I have been preparing you for."

Had God just put me right in my place? With one short sentence, I was reminded that I didn't have to do this alone, that He was right beside me the entire time, and that he knew exactly what the outcome would be. I had years before significantly changed the way I was eating, I was working out, and I was taking supplements that had prepared my body for the physical trauma it was about to endure.

We then proceeded with the preparations after the biopsy. We soon found out that my cultures had been sent to the foremost authority on bone cancer at Johns Hopkins, and he didn't even know what it was. They deemed it "atypical borderline," meaning it was unlikely to recur locally and was not believed to metastasize. So, we were given the option to do nothing, which we viewed as a non-option because there was diseased material inside my leg that shouldn't be there.

The other option was to cut a six- to seven-inch hole in my femur, scrape all of the bad stuff out, put in synthetic material, and cover that hole with a plate secured by seven very long screws that would reach the other side of my bone. Amputation was still on the table, but nobody wanted to do that. Huge plate and long screws it was! We had a plan.

In September of that year, I went in for surgery. I had a real peace about the surgery, and I had accepted that there would be pain. Anyone who has ever had a major surgery knows that gravity is not your friend. As soon as I put that leg down over the side of the bed, I experienced pain I had never felt before. The blood rushed to the bottom of my leg, and it was like somebody took the world's largest jackhammer and just pounded my left leg with it. I couldn't do anything but cry. I was on a walker, wrapped from hip to ankle, and was only allowed to barely touch my toes down on my left leg or toe-touch weight-bearing when I walked. I was essentially walking on one leg. I have never been known for my graceful movements, but it was challenging to maneuver and walk even super short distances. The bathroom in the hospital may have been six steps, but it seemed like 600 miles, and I would cry all the way there and back.

This went on for weeks. The pain was so bad. I couldn't stand it. It would just throb and ache relentlessly. The doctor had given me opioids, but they constipated me terribly and put me to sleep. I know that people become addicted to opioids, but they made me a constipated zombie person. I just wanted to poop, but couldn't. Sometimes being constipated was more terrible than the pain in my leg. So, I was weaned off the medication, and the pain was nothing less than excruciating. I didn't realize that the opioids were just taking the edge off. Bone pain is a whole different animal, unlike anything I had ever felt before.

Physical pain isn't much different from emotional pain in terms of how we move through it. I had to endure the pain to get to the other side. Without pain, there cannot be healing. That has been one of my biggest life lessons. You can't avoid the pain. It's going to be there whether you want it to or not. It's going to come whether you like it or not. It's going to come, whether you're prepared or not. The more tools or strategies you have to cope, the better. The quicker you choose to feel it and move through it, the quicker you heal.

Even after I was off pain meds and able to poop again, I still had to endure daily anticoagulant shots to prevent blood clots. I've always hated needles, and these injections felt like torture. My husband had to administer them because I just couldn't do it myself.

Years later, when I needed injectable peptides to reset my sleep cycle, I found myself paralyzed by the sight of the needles. I couldn't understand why until I realized I had never fully processed the trauma of my surgery. I had been too focused on physical therapy, where, ironically, I found comfort in pain. Pain meant progress, healing, and a light at the end of the tunnel.

Water therapy was supposed to help, but instead, I ended up with a severe foot fungus that nearly reached my ankle. I'll never forget the urgent care doctor recoiling in horror when she saw it. She prescribed every antifungal treatment imaginable, but even after a decade, it still flares up occasionally.

Looking back, I see how much I pushed through without acknowledging my emotional scars. Pain was familiar, so I clung to it, but healing required more than just physical endurance.

I had to start telling myself that it's okay to feel pleasure. It's okay to laugh. It's okay to enjoy yourself. I had a lot of trouble with that after I lost my children because I felt like I shouldn't feel joy. How could I be joyful when my children had passed away? I came to realize that I was punishing myself for something that was not my fault. It was entirely out of my control. It wasn't my fault that we carried a rare gene. That gene had been in both of our families for generations, passed down for decades, and I had no control over that. It wasn't my fault that a tumor grew inside my leg for who knows how long.

I was recently blessed with the opportunity to speak with a woman who had just received a cancer diagnosis similar to mine. When we were introduced, she was still unsure of her plan moving forward to remove her tumor. Through our conversation, we discovered similarities not only in our cancer journeys but also in our life journeys. She needed encouragement and reassurance that her doctors were unable to give her. Only someone who had faced the same challenge could give her the encouragement she was searching for.

That is what this is all about. She needed to hear that while the surgeries were painful, I had persevered. She needed to hear that while my life was put on hold for several months, I returned to life as normal—whatever normal looks like. She needed to hear it as only I could tell it because I lived it ten years ago. I was able to share with her that I did indeed keep my leg. I work out as much and as hard as I want to. I may have to modify certain moves, and my left leg is not as strong as my right, but it doesn't stop me from lifting heavy weights or trying new things. Each of our journeys is unique, and you never know how telling your story can help someone else.

I love hearing others' stories of perseverance and overcoming adversity, but I recently discovered that the most important story I could ever tell is my own. It's helping me heal, but most importantly, talking about my story and writing it down helps me to realize that I have been using tools and strategies all along the way. They developed organically, and some of them from an unhealed place, but they were life-changing nonetheless. It's time to introduce the most transformative framework I use—E.A.T.—in the next chapter.

CHAPTER 12
E.A.T. (EDUCATE-ACCEPT-TRANSFORM)
(CHICKEN VEGETABLE SOUP)

I've always said that if I were a drinker, I'd probably be an alcoholic. But my drug of choice was food. It's what comforted me. It's what took me away from whatever problem I was dealing with at the moment.

However, the E.A.T. Framework was born because I was not only eating my feelings but also trying to educate them away. Let me explain this a little more as we get into the framework.

THE E.A.T FRAMEWORK

Educate

I thought that if I learned more, knew more, had more degrees, and held more certifications, I would mean more. I would mean more to me, and I would mean more to other people. This stems from my desire to make my dad happy, but I realized much later in life that I had to prioritize making myself happy first.

I had to live the life and take the path that God wanted for me—not the path that everyone else had taken or thought that I should be on. I still don't have it all worked out perfectly. I still struggle with impostor syndrome, but I do love to learn.

Education became an obsession or a distraction, just like food, but learning does bring me joy.

I think the most crucial story involving education is Juddsen's, our son. I did not understand how he worked. I needed to know more about what made him tick and what made him explode so that we could motivate him in the proper way, and how we could avoid meltdowns in the appropriate way. I know there are a lot of dedicated parents out there, but I also realize that most parents would not spend almost four years going back to school to get a formal education in order to be able to better raise their child. I understand the gravity of that—and I don't necessarily recommend you do that. It was hard.

It took me away from the very kids I was trying to be a better mother to. But I'm also grateful for that journey. I wouldn't be here today writing this book if I hadn't done it. So I have to be thankful for all of it and know that the way that it flowed and ebbed is precisely how God planned it to be. Educating myself on autism, on other neurodivergent conditions, and just learning more about how the brain works, not only helped me to help my son, but it also helped me to help myself.

Grief and trauma take a toll on the physical body. It's very well-researched these days and is often discussed in the circles I run in, regarding the mind-body connection.[1] It is very real to me. The mind will believe what you tell it to believe. It doesn't distinguish between reality and visualization. But not processing your reality will manifest into physical ailments and symptoms. It wreaks havoc on your nervous system and on your sensory processing. Learning more

---

1. Minnesota Clinic for Health & Wellness, "Understanding the Mind-Body Connection: A Comprehensive Guide," accessed May 13, 2025, https://mnclinic-forhealth.com/understanding-the-mind-body-connection-a-comprehensive-guide/.

about sensory processing also helped me understand how I reacted to things.

I still do not enjoy wearing clothes to this day. Everything bothers me. I feel every piece of clothing on every inch of my body, that it's touching at all times.

It bothers me to put my elbows on the desk or the counter. Sometimes, it even bothers me to hold the steering wheel for a long time. It's not joint pain. It's the actual contact with my skin. It's like I'm having raw nerves. Through education, I have discovered a lot of things that can help or hurt these symptoms. Sleep is crucial, and the food we put into our bodies is essential.

I was very inflamed for a very long time. My son also has trouble with eating, but his issues are sensory-based. He doesn't enjoy the smell of most foods. He doesn't enjoy the way most foods look. He doesn't enjoy the texture of most foods. I'm not sure that he even tastes food the same way that we do because he's already so convinced by the way that it looks and smells of how it is going to taste. Which typically means he will believe that it tastes horrible before ever tasting it at all.

I have tried to get him to try things. We tried watermelon one time. I thought, who doesn't like watermelon? It's great! It's cold, sweet, and refreshing. Well, you know who doesn't like watermelon? Juddsen. He left the room screaming that he had to wash his tongue. You have never seen anything like it.

One time when the kids were younger, we tried to attend a very large church. We were in the back, of course, in case we needed to make an early escape. We had brought some gum, or maybe they were mints. The girls each had one, and so, of course, their little brother wanted to have what his sisters were having. He had never had much candy at that point because he was little, so it was still a choking hazard, but we decided to let him try it. As soon as my husband touched it to Juddsen's tongue, he started bleating like a screaming goat right in the middle of church. All heads turned our way. I was utterly mortified, but to him, it was like a thousand hot pokers on his tongue. He just doesn't feel things the same way that we do.

He can run full speed into a wall and not cry, but if you brush up against his arm, he'll scream at you because you touched him, and he will rub that spot for several minutes. I have learned from raising my son and years working in pediatric occupational therapy that it often seems that people with autism's signals are crossed.

My son loves to be submerged in water, but he hates the feeling of water rolling down his skin. When he was younger, he loved to be wrapped tightly in a blanket or a yoga mat, but screamed inconsolably when wearing footed pajamas. I have learned so much from just raising Juddsen, but my educational background gave me an even deeper understanding and empathy. It also created the willingness to give him extra time or space to avoid certain situations.

Until we really, truly understand something, we can't move past it. You need to have that educational piece in place to accept what is beyond your control. There are a lot of things in this world that are beyond our control. Education also helped me better understand his behaviors and explain why we weren't always willing to join gatherings or participate in community activities.

His nervous system couldn't handle crowded, noisy places for very long or even at all sometimes. And at the time, my nervous system couldn't accommodate his meltdowns without having one of my own. Not everyone is open to hearing the explanation, but those are different stories for a different book. Most people have come to accept Juddsen's shortcomings or quirks after they have better understood his diagnosis. I think this is a lesson for life itself. We often assume things because we don't fully understand a situation. Sometimes we don't want to be educated on the things that scare us because if we don't truly understand, then they aren't happening.

This is denial, not acceptance. You will never be able to accept whatever the challenge is and move through it if you never figure out the circumstances that you can control. When you are fully educated and know exactly what you're up against, it gives you your power back.

I had to do some research on my own when I was diagnosed with a tumor in my leg. I needed to know the possible outcomes. I needed to know the most typical prognosis, but sometimes that can scare you to death, going down the rabbit hole of constant googling. Every case is different, but I needed to understand the surgery so that I could be prepared for the recovery. I couldn't change the fact that I would have to recover, but I could be prepared to take on that challenge.

That's also a significant aspect of personal development. We need to better understand ourselves in order to grow. You must educate yourself on where you are and where you want to be in order to recognize your strengths and areas where you need help. I had to learn who to ask the right questions to. I'm still working on communicating my needs and message in the best way so that others can receive it effectively.

Accept

Acceptance of uncontrollable circumstances can take some time. I felt this most deeply with the rare gene that we carry. This is no one's fault. For a long time, I didn't accept that we couldn't have our own biological children. Looking back now, that is how God intended it to be. We never would have found Juddsen if I had accepted it after we lost our second daughter. But once we had our son DJ, I truly accepted it. It was only then that Juddsen came along. It was similar to our girls as well. It wasn't accepting that we couldn't have our children, but it was accepting that other people could have theirs. I could still love them, and I could still love their children even though I didn't have my own. As soon as I accepted that, my girls came and saved my life.

Acceptance holds an absolute truth in letting go, but not giving up. That's where you have to make the distinction. There are certain things that you can let go of, but that doesn't mean that you're permitting yourself to give up. There are just as many things that are not in your control as things that are in your control. That is where you can genuinely transform the worst and darkest parts of your life into beautiful, beautiful things.

I still sometimes wonder what our biological children would have been like or would have looked like if they had not carried the gene that made them so sick. I adore my kids, and they were meant to be our kids. They are so much like us. There is always a debate about nature versus nurture. Dori is like my husband in so many ways, and Dani is like me in so many ways. Juddsen has our blue eyes, and we're all quirky, just like him. He and I share sensory processing problems, which is probably why I can relate to him so much easier than my husband. Most people would consider us a "perfect" little family.

Transform

It doesn't do you any good to educate yourself and accept the uncontrollable, but not transform it into something new. We're all here to help each other. We're all here to lift each other up. My most valuable lessons have come from my most challenging times. My most profound moments of awakening came from being consumed by despair. I don't think you can truly understand what it means to feel renewed unless you have lost a part of yourself.

I don't wish tragedy upon anyone, and I also don't believe that you need to experience tragedy to build something beautiful. But some of us are harder-headed than others. We need a swifter kick in the pants. As humans, we love a good comeback story, right? I love to read books about people's life stories and how they overcame adversity.

Even though I lived through my story, it's my story. Some of its magnificence and miracle is lost on me. When I can see it through someone else's lens and understand the potential it has to help that person, it fuels me to keep sharing it. Someone else living through some of the same circumstances may be able to get up after the twenty-seventh time she was knocked down because she heard my story.

I thank God and my support system for being with me all along the way, for having patience with me, and for encouraging me. God has shown me big and small miracles throughout my life. I have come to expect them, and I pray that you can too.

I'm going to leave some space in the following few pages to go through the E.A.T. framework. Take one or two situations in your life. Write down the situation or challenge. List some of the ways you can educate yourself to better understand the problem you are facing. In the case of betrayal, such as I experienced with my husband's infidelity, I had to educate myself on my part in the story. What was I doing or not doing that helped to lead to that infidelity? I'm not making excuses for him, but marriage takes two people, and I was not holding up my end of our vows. I needed to understand why I was behaving the way I was. We needed to communicate with each other to understand what the other person needed. I had to accept and forgive. It happened. I couldn't change that. But by moving through that together, we created a marriage that is stronger now than it ever has been. You can apply this to any situation in your life, big or small.

Write down what it is you need to understand and how you can better be educated on that problem or challenge. Then, make two lists under the acceptance portion. One list of things that you cannot control and one list of things you can take control of right now.

The transformation portion is the fun part. Write down dreams, goals, or wishes that you would like to see come out of your hard situation. What could it truly become? My son's diagnosis gave me an entirely new career path and the opportunity to help other families and their children. My tumor surgeries led me to pour myself into fitness and nutrition, and go on to become a certified fitness and nutrition coach to help other women.

If my husband had never cheated on me, I wouldn't have had the opportunity to transform our marriage. It wouldn't be the beautiful thing that it is now, and we probably wouldn't be as close to God and keep God in our marriage like we do now.

Every dark thing can be brought into the light. **Please take the time to complete this exercise** now or later, and use these tools to support you in all your future challenges.

_____

_____

_____

_____

_____

_____

_____

_____

_____

EAT YOUR FEELINGS

CHAPTER 13
THE F.O.O.D. FRAMEWORK
(STUFFED BELL PEPPERS)

My relationship with food was unhealthy from a young age. The fleeting feeling of comfort that I would experience from food when I was upset or emotionally unstable made me want to try to recreate that feeling again and again. The problem was that I was looking for comfort and validation from outside sources, and it all stemmed from not loving myself. This relationship with ourselves is the most important but most often overlooked.

I have discussed relationships extensively throughout this book because that is something I struggle with. I was never led to believe as a child that I was enough, that I was good at the things that I did, or that the ideas I had were worth hearing. I've done a lot of soul-searching, and I realize now that that's not true, but I have been in that belief system for so many years that it can creep up and creep out. I have to remind myself that I have always been enough, just as I am. No human being can change that.

Just like my relationship with food was warped pretty early in life so was anything to do with fitness. I ran track. I played softball and soccer, but I never really felt like I was a part of the team. This never had anything to do with my teammates. I was never bullied or deliberately left out of anything. The negative self-talk and dislike that I felt for myself was worse than anything anyone else could say or do to me. I was so insecure and so afraid of not doing anything right that I would choose not to do anything at all—at that time, not putting forth much of an effort meant not failing. I now completely understand that the only time you fail is when you don't try. I'm still trying to teach my kids this concept to this very day.

Despite all my insecurities, I played sports anyway, mostly because Dad told me to. However, I was actually pretty fast. I could run around the bases during softball faster than most of my teammates. I looked a little funny doing it, but that's okay. I could chase a ball down in the outfield like nobody's business. I could throw the softball from the fence in the outfield and land a one-hopper to home plate. I ran all the shorter races on the track and could hold my own. I never won an individual race (that I recall), but I was part of some winning relay teams. I liked the 200-meter and the 400-meter relays. I could never work up enough speed in enough time to run the 100 meters.

But no matter what I did, it was never good enough for my dad. In some ways, that drove me to overachieve. I was good at school. My brain was always my biggest muscle. I used to have a near-photographic memory. I would write, rewrite, and rewrite my notes. So, when I would take a test, I could see the page of notes in my head. I could pick out the answer from the notes that I saw in my head.

I didn't understand or even know about the mind-body connection back then. There was a disconnect, which just got worse as my trauma compounded. In my adulthood, I have focused particularly on the brain-body connection, the mind-muscle connection, and the mental health-gut connection. The moral of the story is that everything is connected. My first lesson on that came in indoor soccer. When I fractured my collarbone, I learned that everything is connected. This can also be true in life itself. Decisions made early in life can affect outcomes later in life. Mistakes made in a marriage can affect the relationship in the future. Interestingly enough, my husband getting off track in our marriage was the turning point in me focusing on my self-care.

His infidelity made me realize that I had to learn how to love myself if I was going to be able to love my family the way I needed to. Just as I did with everything else, I went a little overboard. It all started with online workouts. Are you familiar with the original Tony Horton workouts? We loved Tony Horton back in those days, and his workouts were challenging. I felt accomplished whenever I would do one of them.

Then I decided that I needed a more community-oriented approach. Online communities are fantastic, but it is when you get in the room with those same people that the magic happens. That is why I started working out at the gym, and it was like nothing else I had experienced. I made so many friends. I adored the trainer I had at that time. I secretly always wanted to be a trainer. It started back in high school when I had my first knee surgery, and the physical therapist helped me overcome the worst pain I had experienced in my life to that point. I loved the relationship that formed between therapist and patient, much like trainer and athlete.

There is a much deeper relationship with a trainer than with workouts. It's about more than just building muscle or enhancing your endurance. It can come with real lessons that spill over into other parts of your life. You are pushing your body beyond its limits, challenging what you believe it can do. My trainer was an excellent motivator. He believes that everybody can be an athlete. He doesn't care what size, shape, color, height, or weight you were when you started. He only believes that you could do more than you had been doing.

That's why I enjoyed his bootcamp-style workouts for so long. They made me feel empowered and strong. Lifting heavy weights calms my nervous system. I love to pick up heavy things and put them down on repeat. I also enjoy yoga, Pilates, and mobility, but I don't enjoy running unless I'm trying to get away from something. I do HIIT (high-intensity interval training) because I know that it is beneficial a couple of days a week, but it is not because I enjoy it.

After my leg surgery, my leg did not enjoy running or HIIT. It still doesn't enjoy those activities. Walking outside, however, is great for all my senses. The bottom line is that moving your body is important, and it can be very calming to your nervous system. So, I was officially obsessed with working out, but I still had that unhealthy relationship with food.

I couldn't find a good balance between working out and nutrition that worked efficiently with my body. I could either focus on my nutrition, or I could focus on my workouts—but not both at the same time. Remember the mental health-gut connection we discussed earlier? My weight yo-yoed for years. I have gained and lost the same thirty pounds at least four times. The current program I coach is the only one I have ever been able to sustain and feel successful in both my workouts and nutrition. Find out more about The FasterWay to Fat Loss from the link on my website; just scan the QR code at the beginning or end of the book.

But before I found The FasterWay, I started to realize that the empowering boot camp-style workouts I was addicted to were tough on my body. They were affecting my sleep. My cortisol levels were skewed, and unbeknownst to me at the time, I was entering perimenopause in my late thirties. I have been in fight-or-flight mode my entire life, so I tend to stay there. There would be some nights when I would do boot camp, and I would not sleep. My whole body would buzz. Literally, everything hurt.

Timing workouts and food was also very confusing to me back then, and I often ate when I wasn't hungry. Why was I eating when I was stressed, sad, or even angry? I turned to food for comfort, but it started a vicious cycle of shame and guilt, which led to more eating for comfort. It seemed impossible to break until I learned to sit with the feelings that I was trying to "eat." I had to give them space, let them be heard, and understand what was making me want to eat.

That's why I created the F.O.O.D. framework.

THE F.O.O.D. FRAMEWORK

Feel

You have to feel the emotion driving your need to eat—determine if you are truly hungry or if it's something else. As I discussed in Chapter 6, anxiety makes me crave crunchy or salty foods. Sadness often leads to a craving for something sweet, such as cake or pudding, or cake with pudding in the middle! Anger evokes the need to feel comforted with something hot, like a thick chili. Sometimes I stand in the pantry looking at the food that I want to eat and ask myself, "Why do you want to eat those sweet potato chips?"

Granted, I do make healthier choices these days. Before, I would eat half a box of Cheez-Its or half a bag of Cheeto Puffs. Now, if I still feel the need to eat when I'm anxious, I grab some organic sweet potato chips or seeded, organic, gluten-free crackers. They have no artificial ingredients, but still fill my need in the moment.

Option

You have the option to change the way that you feel about something at any given moment. *You* control your feelings. *You* tell your brain what to think, and *you* need to take back that control. Remember that. I may want to eat those chips because I am nervous, but I would be better served if I turned that anxiety into excitement about an upcoming event. You can choose to release the feeling altogether or take control of it and give it a new name. Listen to your body, understand the feeling, and then control your brain to control your body.

Observe

Observe how that shift changed your mindset. I can break myself of a craving pretty fast. Some feelings are deeper than others, and I need to distract myself. I may go for a walk. I may drink some coffee. I may drink some water. I may just close the door of the pantry. However, I also take note of what worked or didn't work the last time I felt that particular way. If you try to flip the script on your mind and it backfires on you, observe that. If it's too forced and you can't truly believe it, then it won't shift your mindset.

Don't be discouraged if you aren't entirely successful the first or second time you try this method. It does take a little practice, but once you feel the shift, it should only take you a few minutes, or even a few seconds, to run through the process the next time.

This takes us to the last step.

Decide or Deprive

Once I have completed those first three steps, I can exercise the option to reclaim my power. I decide if I still want to eat the food or not. Or I distract myself with an energy-invoking activity. It can be okay to give in to a craving if it is something that your body really needs. Just like I can decide to eat a few sweet potato chips, if I want chocolate, I may just eat a small piece of dark chocolate. It may be better to give in to a small indulgence instead of setting off an avalanche of eating. Avoiding the craving altogether may result in eating several other things instead of just having a tiny indulgence.

You want to get to the place where you can have a treat, or you can go ahead and eat your feelings on a smaller scale. This can help you avoid the snowball effect, where you can't stop eating. That's where I used to be. I used to start with a bag of chips, and then I would go to the cookies, and then I would have popcorn. It would quickly get out of control.

The F.O.O.D. framework is designed to help you get to the root of your emotional eating, allowing you to reclaim your power. The real win is the power in the pause. Pausing for a moment breaks that mindless eating. Mindless eating is survival mode eating. I want for you to feel the shift; to feel the power of the pause so that you can start stacking those little wins.

Fitness and nutrition are not just about physical health. It starts with a mindset, and it has to be a lifestyle, not a diet. I have tried almost every diet under the sun. I used to eat tuna, cottage cheese, half an apple, and five saltine crackers for five to seven days to drop ten pounds. It was a fad diet that several friends and I would do together back in the day. That's probably why I don't eat too much tuna to this day. It would just grow in my mouth, this big wad of tuna, and I couldn't stand to eat it any longer.

I've done keto, the Mediterranean diet, and liquid diets. I've tried just about every protein shake on the internet. But one of the biggest game changers for me was cutting out gluten and dairy. They are so inflammatory to my body.[1] I realized this after cutting them out of my diet and noticing the difference it made—my bloating decreased, my skin improved, and my joints stopped hurting. This may not be true for everyone, but it is true for me. I have known for a long time that I was lactose intolerant, but I didn't realize it until I was in my thirties. There were so many things that I didn't figure out until later in life. I want you to learn from my mistakes. I totally get that some of this can seem overwhelming. I understand that life is busy.

But, Benjamin Franklin said it best. "If you fail to plan, you are planning to fail." You have to have some kind of plan for your nutrition, or you will end up eating whatever is in front of you.

Don't make it complicated. I eat a lot of the same things every day. That makes it simple, especially during the week, so I don't have

---

[1]. "Here's What a Dietitian Says About Dairy Causing Inflammation," *EatingWell*, October 14, 2019, https://www.eatingwell.com/article/2056066/heres-what-a-dietitian-says-about-dairy-causing-inflammation/.

to stress about it. Taking the stress out allowed me to change my perception of planning and ultimately changed my relationship with food.

I see it as fuel for my body and protein to build the muscles I want. I think that's just a good lesson for life. To feel more positive toward anything, you must build a positive relationship with it. That is why I have been working on loving myself for the past ten years. I can say that I love myself now, and I could not say that before. I love the person that I'm becoming. I love that I want to help people. I love that I can say that I love myself.

When you love yourself, you are more committed to taking care of not only your mind but also your body. Whether we like it or not, they will always be connected. So we have to feed both of them. We have to nurture both of them. We must continue to grow both of them.

Writing this book has been so fun. Well, not everything has been fun, but it has definitely been cathartic. We are almost at the last chapter. I thought that I would be so excited to be at the end, but I'm a little bit sad that I'm nearly done with this book. Enjoy the last super short chapter, and I hope to get to meet you, either on social media or at a book signing!

CHAPTER 14
THIS IS NOT THE LAST CHAPTER
(PINEAPPLE UPSIDE DOWN CAKE)

I can't believe that I made it to the last chapter! But this is not the last chapter for me or you. This book has been on my heart for the good part of fifteen years, but my trauma started well before that, when I was a child. If any part of my story resonated with you, I hope you're able to take away at least one of the lessons I learned or frameworks I use. I have had many addictions over the years—food, knowledge, working out, and even pain. Addiction may look different for you, but healing doesn't have to. We cannot bury our feelings with addiction.

The power of perseverance lives inside all of us. It isn't saved for those more qualified or more deserving. It is available to all of us at any given moment. The key is getting to the root of the problem or the solution. It is there that you decide whether to cultivate that root so that it can grow or pull it out, never to be replanted.

I pray that this book has helped you. I pray that you are committed to healing yourself. If you are already on the path of healing, I pray that you will commit to helping other people find their way to that path as well. In every trial, there is a lesson. In every lesson, there is a purpose. I am not certain of my next steps on this journey, but I am confident that I will take them one foot in front of the other. I believe that our steps are ordered, and sometimes we have to keep walking even if we can't see the path clearly—or that there is a path at all.

I would love to hear your story of perseverance and your next steps. Thank you for reading and for being a part of my story. It means more to me and my family than you could ever know.

ACKNOWLEDGMENTS

This book can't be completely finished without saying a few heartfelt thank yous.

First to my husband, who has been my loudest cheerleader and my greatest support system for half of my life. I don't have enough words to thank him properly. I will love you forever!

Thank you to my kids, who have put up with all of my "personalities" over the years and continued to love me no matter how I may have treated them. Please know that I was always doing my very best and that wasn't always good enough.

Thank you Mom, my sisters, and my in-laws, for accepting all of my flaws and loving me through every heartbreak and every accomplishment.

Thank you Dad, God rest your soul, for loving me the best way you knew how and supporting me now from the afterlife.

Thank you to my unstoppable community for believing in me and never thinking that any dream was too big to accomplish!

Thank you to my developmental editor, Jenny and the entire Game Changer Publishing team. I couldn't have done this without you!!

Finally, thank you Jesus for walking with me hand in hand through my trials and lending me your Faith when mine wavered.

THANK YOU FOR READING MY BOOK!

Just to say thanks for buying and reading my book, I would like to invite you to my free online community, no strings attached!

Scan the QR Code:

I appreciate your interest in my book and value your feedback as it helps me improve future versions of this book. I would appreciate it if you could leave your invaluable review on Amazon.com with your feedback. Thank you!

www.ingramcontent.com/pod-product-compliance
Lightning Source LLC
Chambersburg PA
CBHW030247010526
44107CB00031B/1349/J